I have been on my halftime journey for over a decade. This current season has felt a bit dry—I drank this book in. It was just what the doctor ordered!

LINDA REEB, founder of MomsMentoring.com and coauthor of *Halftime for Couples*

Your best is yet to come! Don't believe me? Read *Women at Halftime* and you'll learn, just as I did several years ago, that God has so much more for you—things beyond your wildest imagination! Don't resign or retire . . . re*fire*! This book will help you become all God created *you* to be.

DIANE SPICER, author of *Unmasked: A Remarkable True Story of Transformation and Redemption* and Halftime Australia executive coach

Once when I was challenged to visualize an image that depicted my purpose, I imagined a suspension swinging bridge over a river gorge. The choice is yours: Stay where you are, known and safe, or dare to step toward a new future. *Women at Halftime* is the suspension bridge for all who read it.

SANDRA L. FRAZIER, MD, UAB Medicine Provider health officer

Carolyn and Shayne not only identify the possible directions for your life, but they also lay out guidelines to facilitate your journey. Relatable life lessons demonstrate the ability to transform dreams and passions into a fulfilling life. This is the ultimate "pay it forward" book, and the authors' enthusiasm, faith, and focus are infectious.

KATHY ANDERSON

Women at Halftime is incredible. It was like the book was written for me. The three words *pray*, *act*, and *adjust*—along with *forgive*—are the most powerful words in the book. Whoever reads this book will not be disappointed!

LAURA CONTRERAS ROWE, author, entrepreneur, and Realtor

This wonderful book provides the tools, quiet challenge of reflection, and encouragement for every woman to let God help her finish well. Grab a cup of tea and settle in for a life-changing read!

> **JO ANNA COUCH**, MS, CPC, owner of Coaching by Faith, a Christian executive/life coaching practice

Women at Halftime addresses the diverse challenges encountered by women in midlife. Utilizing the tools and plans provided and embracing God's calling in our lives, we can feel supported and encouraged by other women's wisdom and experiences.

> **JULIE ANDERSON**, broker-owner, AFJ Properties

I started as a Fellow of the Halftime Institute in August 2020—the year the world experienced a lockdown due to COVID and the year I turned fifty. As a senior corporate executive who travels more than 50 percent of each year for a global multinational, I found 2020 to be almost like a divine pause year, giving me time to reflect, *What is my calling for Life 2.0?* In fact, being the only Asian and woman among my esteemed colleagues of American men, I asked HTI, Where are all the women attendees at Halftime? So I am super glad this book is finally published for women who are entering halftime. Ladies, the best part of your life is yet to be.

> **JULIENNE LOH**, Halftime Fellow 2020, Singapore

As a former participant of the Halftime Institute, I was pleasantly surprised to see how *Women of Halftime* challenged me to continue my journey to relevance. The authors weave personal stories with tools for introspection and challenging exercises to prompt further growth. Whether you have determined your relevance or are still searching your soul, this book will help you come to conclusions about yourself and your future.

> **ELLEN VOIE**, CAE and president/CEO of Women In Trucking Association, Inc.

As my children started to leave the nest, I soon realized a whole new world of significance was awaiting me outside the home. Halftime Institute was a key help to get me started on a new calling and career of significance. *Women at Halftime* is the perfect guide for women pursuing their halftime calling.

MARGARET ERENETA, Halftime Institute graduate and producer of *One80 Podcast*

Women at Halftime shows how to make the next season of life even more purposeful by boldly giving women the courage to dream, providing a systematic way to rediscover our gifts and identify our values, and granting the freedom to dig up the buried treasures of our true selves. The authors share an easy-to-follow method of emotional and spiritual management, while helping us always keep our focus on Scripture and our eyes fixed on Christ.

ASHLEY NORONHA, cofounder of The Truth & Beauty Project

What if a vibrant life—one that God uniquely created you to live out—awaited you in your next season? Would you be willing to be vulnerable and intentional as you spend time with the Lord to bask in such a season? If so, then come journey with Shayne and Carolyn as they walk you through a wonderful balance of Scripture, guidance, encouragement, and next steps to get you going into your next season . . . one that he has handcrafted for you, his cherished daughter.

CARRIE PARK, wife, mother of five, leader, writer, and speaker

Women at Halftime offers an inspiring road map for women at midlife who want more—more purpose and impact—but aren't sure how to get there. The book offers a proven process intermixed with encouraging stories and practical steps. What an invitation to purpose and joy for the next season of life!

WENDE GAIKEMA, executive coach and principal, Coach Wende

This beautiful book is long overdue. Yet the wait has resulted in a rich treasure of practical, prayerful, and purposeful tools and stories that could not have sparkled years ago. May we all ponder anew what God has for us next.

SHARLA LANGSTON, cofounder and advisory council, Women Doing Well

Though the central premises of halftime are not gender-specific, *Women at Halftime* embraces the female perspective. This book provides the perfect road map: how to thoughtfully assess your day-to-day activities, spend time figuring out who you are and what you can do, and keep working in that direction. Most importantly, don't do it alone; God will provide resources and relationships just when you need them!

MARY LONG

Women *at* Halftime

Foreword
by Margie
Blanchard

A Guide to Reigniting Dreams *and* Finding
Renewed Joy and Purpose in Your Next Season

Women *at* Halftime

Shayne Moore *and* Carolyn Castleberry Hux
A HALFTIME INSTITUTE RESOURCE

TYNDALE
MOMENTUM

A Tyndale nonfiction imprint

Visit Tyndale online at tyndale.com.

Visit Tyndale Momentum online at tyndalemomentum.com.

Tyndale, Tyndale's quill logo, *Tyndale Momentum*, and the Tyndale Momentum logo are registered trademarks of Tyndale House Ministries. Tyndale Momentum is a nonfiction imprint of Tyndale House Publishers, Carol Stream, Illinois.

Women at Halftime: A Guide to Reigniting Dreams and Finding Renewed Joy and Purpose in Your Next Season

Cover designed by Faceout Studios, Lindy Martin

Edited by Christine M. Anderson

The authors are represented by the Gates Group, www.the-gates-group.com.

Note: The names and details of some clients have been changed to protect privacy.

For information about special discounts for bulk purchases, please contact Tyndale House Publishers at csresponse@tyndale.com, or call 1-855-277-9400.

Library of Congress Cataloging-in-Publication Data

A catalog record for this book is available from the Library of Congress.

ISBN 978-1-4964-5237-5

Printed in the United States of America

28	27	26	25	24	23	22
7	6	5	4	3	2	1

This book is dedicated to our daughters:
Greta and Elizabeth
Lindsay, Brooke, Rachel, and Kara

Keep it safe
Let no one drown it out
Your voice and light
Erase all doubt

CONTENTS

AN INVITATION TO RENEWED PURPOSE AND JOY

Margie Blanchard

Women at Halftime is a gift—for you, for someone you love, for a women's support group, for every woman at midlife who wants to recapture her spark of purpose and joy. This helpful, well-researched work develops and extends the halftime ideas pioneered nearly thirty years ago by Bob Buford and applies them to the unique challenges of women in midlife—a time when they have more opportunities than ever before. If only they knew which ones to take and which would fit their unique abilities and situation. If only they had help in engineering the necessary changes.

Getting to know Bob Buford and spending quality time with him was one of the great blessings of my life. Serving on the boards of the Leadership Network and the Halftime Institute for many years, as well as going through eighteen months of halftime coaching myself, deepened that blessing. Because the majority of those attending Halftime Institute programs were men, those of us on the board often wondered, "Do the women in our programs need something different than what we offer men?" For example, I had heard one female executive say she had three times as many stakeholders in her life as the men she knew, and each of those stakeholders would be significantly impacted if she made *any* changes in her life. We also discovered that the early tagline and promise of halftime, "moving from success to significance," did not resonate with many women who felt their years of caring for home, hearth, and children were of utmost significance.

What makes *Women at Halftime* different from many other life- and career-planning guides is that God is at the center of it. The promise of Ephesians 2:10—that we are God's workmanship and created for good works—is the central principle for this work.

I love how Shayne and Carolyn recommend doing this half-time work over time and with others—a coach, mentor, friend, or small group. Invite someone to join you as you begin this journey. Then get ready to see your life change as the authors lead you through the four stages: Get Clear, Get Free, Get Called, and Get Going. This is not a process that can happen in a couple of days or even weeks. The goal is not a quick fix but a long-term one to help you find joy and fulfillment to sustain you throughout your second half. Beginning with the foundation of positive experiences that have led up to midlife, Shayne and Carolyn build on who you are and what you've learned and accomplished to help launch you into something meaningful and enjoyable for your next season—a season God cares deeply about! If you're looking for renewed purpose and joy, I can think of no better guide than *Women at Halftime.*

WELCOME TO HALFTIME

"My best years are behind me."

"Nobody knows what to do with a fifty-year-old housewife trying to reenter the workforce. I can't make it past the human resources department because they have no idea what to do with me. I feel worthless."

"I focused on my career and never married or had children. Now that my career is ending, I feel completely lost. Who am I?"

"I am ready for more, but I don't know where to even begin to find it."

"I want to work but I feel like the world has passed me by. I loved raising my children and volunteering at church, but those things did not prepare me for my second half."

"I feel like God is finished with me."

If you resonate with any of these statements, chances are you are in a place we call "halftime"—a disorienting midlife transition for which no one prepared you. What was most significant in your first half of life either no longer fits or no longer even exists. The children you raised have left the nest or soon will. The career or volunteer work that once gave you fulfillment and significance no longer brings you joy. A foundational relationship that once gave you a sense of identity or belonging ended in divorce, death, or relational breakdown. Or it may be that you simply have a gnawing sense that something is missing in your life. Whatever the road that led you to halftime, the daunting question is, "What now?"

Our promise to you is that there is an answer to that question, one that is as unique as you are. As challenging as it may seem right now, your halftime season is actually a gift—a time to discover a new source of energy and significance for your next season. Just as sports teams take a halftime break to regroup in the locker room and strategize with their coach, your midlife transition is a time to pause and strategize for a winning second half.

We can promise that there is a way through the disorientation of midlife because we have both navigated our own halftime crises and discovered new callings on the other side. Based on our experiences as well as those of many other women we've coached, we wrote *Women at Halftime* to walk you through a tried-and-true process for getting unstuck and finding renewed joy and purpose in your second half.

THE UNIQUE CHALLENGES OF WOMEN AT MIDLIFE

It's likely no surprise to you that midlife is full of unique challenges for women. These include navigating changes in family relationships, balancing work and personal life, rediscovering self, securing enough resources, coping with loss and transition, managing health problems, and dealing with menopause.[1] However, what you may not know is that midlife and menopause themselves are relatively recent experiences for women.

Dr. Louann Brizendine, author of *The Female Brain*, points out that a century ago, menopause was rare because the life expectancy of women in the United States was forty-nine, two years before the average woman begins to experience menopause.[2] Today, life expectancy for women in the US is just over eighty years,[3] which means most of us will live decades after ending our menstrual cycles. It also means that empty nesting and the need to plan for the years after menopause are, historically speaking, recent challenges for women. Which helps explain in part why science, psychology, culture, and the church have largely failed to catch up with this reality. Today, as millions of us approach and live beyond this once rare female transition, there are relatively few resources available to help us navigate the unique challenges we face. Researchers on the topic admit,

> We remain relatively uninformed about the unique experiences of midlife women. Given the recognition of midlife as a stage of the lifespan in which important transitions occur, it is surprising that little attention has been focused on understanding the consequences of stress and women's mental health. . . .
>
> As seen in research on other portions of the lifespan, many of the instruments developed to study stress in men are not adequate for studying women.[4]

And the findings of the research that has been done on women and midlife is sobering. Women face some of their greatest mental health risks during midlife.

- A recent study by the Centers for Disease Control and Prevention found that one in eight middle-aged women in the United States has depression, which is the highest rate of depression among any age or gender group.[5]

- Another study found that the suicide rate for middle-aged women has increased by 63 percent since 1999.[6]

- A study on happiness in 132 countries found that unhappiness in developed countries peaks at around age 47.[7]

These mental health struggles are only compounded by other challenges common at midlife, which include crippling debts, crumbling relationships, feeling left behind at work, empty nests or unlaunched children, and caring for aging parents. All of it leaves many middle-aged women feeling that life is an unending burden.[8] It also demonstrates how difficult this season really is. The struggle is real! To navigate midlife well, women need resources that are not only tailored to their unique needs and challenges, but ones that also draw on the experiences and wisdom of other women. And that is why we wrote *Women at Halftime*.

THE UNIQUE NEEDS OF WOMEN AT HALFTIME

Women at Halftime traces its origins to the work of the Halftime Institute and its founder, Bob Buford. Following the 1994 publication of his bestselling book, *Halftime: Moving from Success to Significance*, Bob founded the Halftime Institute to provide guidance and coaching for others who were walking through their own midlife transitions. Most of those who participated in the institute's programs were men, so the curriculum reflected their needs and experiences. As more women began to join their ranks over the years, it became apparent that women at midlife had unique needs that weren't being addressed.

- Many women did not relate to the assumption behind the institute's long-standing tagline "from success to significance," especially when they had sacrificed careers to raise children. For some, a better tagline might have been "from sacrifice to significance." Other women were offended by the tagline because they felt raising their children was the most significant thing they had done or ever would do. Having started with significance in their first half, they felt they were losing it at halftime when their children left the nest.

- While men typically found it easy to identify a dream for their second half, many women did not. Women who had turned off their dreamer to empower the career of a husband or to support the aspirations of their children often struggled to turn their dreamer back on again once they had a chance. In fact, many actually felt afraid to dream again.

- Because the starting point for most men was "success," they typically began their halftime journeys with baseline emotional assets such as confidence, pride in accomplishments, and perseverance. In contrast, women tended to come to halftime feeling at a deficit and burdened by negative emotions such as emptiness, discouragement, and hopelessness.

In response to feedback from women, the Halftime Institute first solicited input from an advisory group of female alumni and leaders, and then commissioned a survey to collect more information. As the energy for this new initiative continued to build, Halftime Institute leaders asked for volunteers who would be willing to go deeper by gathering stories to learn more about how to better meet the unique needs of women at halftime. We raised our hands to volunteer, and that's when the book you now hold in your hands began to take shape.[9]

More than one hundred women shared their stories with us. Some were interviewed by Carolyn, and some wrote out their stories for us. Others shared their stories with Shayne as they traveled with her on a vision trip to Africa in search of new purpose. As we began to write, still others shared their struggles and broken dreams as well as their breakthroughs and new dreams. What emerged was an inspiring, collective story of women who bravely navigated their halftime challenges and changed their futures. It's a story we're eager to share with you.

OUR HOPE FOR YOU

Our hope is that as you engage with us and this process, you will emerge on the other side with renewed confidence and purpose. The promise of this book is that God still has work for you to do, and his dreams and plans for you are bigger, better, and more significant than anything you could come up with on your own. There is hope for your future. You are not done.

In the pages that follow, we'll lead you through a four-stage process to help you get unstuck and moving toward your dreams. The four stages, which are reflected in the four-part structure of the book, are Get Clear, Get Free, Get Called, and Get Going. We'll talk more about each stage in chapter 1. We share stories from our own halftime journeys, and each of the four parts opens with a brief vignette from Shayne's halftime journey. We'll also introduce you to women who have walked this same path ahead of you. While each woman worked through the same four-part process to get unstuck, each one also discovered renewed joy and purpose in her own unique way. We believe the same will be true for you.

To help you keep moving through the process, each chapter includes guidance and exercises for self-discovery and application. Some activities will be fairly easy to implement, and others will require more time and work. There is no set time frame for your journey, and no gold stars for rushing through it. Each stage builds on the one before it, so we encourage you to take the time you need to work through it. Because halftime is a journey of self-discovery, it's also important to write down what you're learning and feeling as you go. Using a journal throughout will give you a treasure trove of resources to draw on as you chart your course.

We encourage you to invite a friend or a group of women to take this journey with you. The wisdom of Scripture is, "Two people are better off than one, for they can help each other succeed. . . . Three are even better, for a triple-braided cord is not easily broken" (Ecclesiastes 4:9, 12). You may also find it helpful to process your journey with a certified coach, counselor, pastor, or spiritual director. Women are at their best when they are in safe and nurturing relationships with others. If you tend to isolate or withdraw when you are struggling, we invite you to take the risk of inviting at least one other person to travel with you during this season. It could make all the difference.

We believe a meaningful and abundant life is available to you in your second half, and we are eager to help you explore your identity and values, discover your strengths and spiritual gifts, leave behind fear and limitations, and awaken to your truest self, grounded in Christ. We invite you to join us to Get Clear on who you are and who you are not, to Get Free of what is holding you back, to Get Called by God, and to Get Going into a second half of joy and purpose.

Welcome to halftime.

1

EMBRACE CHANGE

We don't change when we are comfortable. It comes with pain.
That's the nature of the beast of transition.

MICHELLE KILBOURNE, PHD

CAROLYN

I believed my life was over, and I could feel my spirit dying. Falling to the floor in my bedroom, I begged God to show up.

"Where are you, Lord?" I cried. "Do you see what is happening? Do you care?"

The life I had so carefully planned and cultivated was ending, along with my marriage of more than two decades. Although I had seen the end coming for years, it happened just as my children were leaving the nest. In fact, my goal had been to hold everything together until the kids were safely away at college so they wouldn't have to deal with the daily realities of a broken family. If they didn't have to live through the ending, I hoped they wouldn't feel the loss as deeply. I was wrong.

I gave God an earful that day. Like so many women, I had

sacrificed my full-time career to work as a hybrid mom, staying at home and building a flexible work life around my children's schedules. Now, my marriage of twenty-four years was over, my children had flown the nest, and I was approaching my fifties feeling overwhelmed by abandonment and loss. On top of everything else, I had scant evidence God cared about my life.

I tried to look toward the future, but I was haunted by doubts. *Is my life over? What purpose do I still have? Are my best years behind me?*

As I lay there on the floor yell-praying, I felt powerless and invisible. And yet, it was in that dark place that God met me. I heard no booming voices from heaven, and there were no bright lights or angel visitations. I simply felt God's Spirit move in my heart and soul as I poured out my lament of disappointments.

"Finish what you started in me, God," I prayed. "Your love is eternal—don't quit on me now." It was a simple prayer in the midst of this heartbreaking season of change, but it was all I could muster in the moment. It must have been enough. Miraculously, a faint flicker of hope stirred in me, and it was sufficient to get me up off the floor to take my first step. Then another and another.

THE FIRST STEP FROM CRISIS TO ABUNDANT LIFE

If you are a woman at midlife, chances are you have experienced something similar. What was most significant in the first half of your life is either gone or no longer feels like enough. Your life may have revolved around raising children, and now you are an empty nester asking, "What's next?" You may be nearing the end of a successful career, or in a ministry position that no longer fits your giftings, passions, or calling. You may have sacrificed much in the first half of life to pursue a career, a relationship, or a family life you found rewarding. Now, however, whatever you sacrificed for has changed, ended, or no longer feels rewarding. So today, you are looking for a new kind of significance, a new source of energy and joy for your next season.

The stories and circumstances of women at halftime may be different, but the range of emotions we experience in this difficult season are shared by women everywhere. It's as if we have fallen down a deep well and there is no way out. We struggle as we face transitions we may or may not have chosen. We wrestle with feelings of intellectual, spiritual, and emotional emptiness. We grieve the loss of significant relationships and may feel lonely, disconnected, or isolated. We might sense a vague discontent or feel that we have no sense of purpose at all.

Shayne and I understand the fear and confusion of midlife. We both went through halftime crises and found renewed purpose to navigate our next seasons of life. I found my second-half calling as a coach for the Halftime Institute and had the honor of walking with Shayne through her own valley of despair. Today, we call each other friends and work collaboratively to share what we've learned to help other women. In the pages that follow, we share our stories and the stories of others who have navigated the disorientation of halftime and come through it with renewed purpose. Our hope is to help you move from the crises and challenges of midlife to a meaningful and abundant life.

There is a pathway to joy and significance in your next season,

"I feel like it's time to make my life count, time to find my passions and set new priorities. But I'm also scared because I'm not sure how to get back out there after serving my family and church for decades."

Karen Volpert, MA, Sotheby's Institute of Art, London

and this book will guide you through it. However, taking this journey requires something of you. You must be willing to not only make some changes here and there, but to also embrace change as a lifestyle. It's a decision that only you can make. My own halftime coach put it to me this way: "The first step to changing your life is realizing that you are responsible for your life. You're responsible for where you are now and for where you will go next."

FOUR TRANSFORMATIONAL STAGES

Over the years of coaching hundreds of women, we've discovered that the process of getting unstuck and finding new joy and peace includes four transformational stages: Get Clear, Get Free, Get Called, and Get Going. Each stage builds on the one before it, beginning with the foundation of Get Clear.

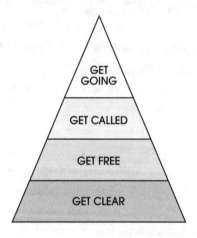

Get Clear requires doing the hard work of identifying not only who you are today, but also who you are *not*. The purpose of the Get Clear stage is to excavate your past, pay attention to the reality of your present, and begin imagining your new future. This stage is about getting clarity on both your true identity in God and what you value most at this stage of life.

Get Free is about breaking away from whatever keeps you from fulfilling the dreams you have for your life or from dreaming at all. This stage is about leaving behind limiting beliefs, facing fears, and creating capacity and space in your life for change.

Get Called is not about merely finding a better life—something you can create on your own—it's about discovering God's best for you. Finding your second-half calling requires listening to God as well as listening to your life. The goal of this stage is to identify what God has uniquely prepared you to do and what he is calling you to do.

Get Going is the stage in which you begin to take tangible steps toward change. Building on the previous three stages, this one is about persevering through setbacks and confusion as you pursue a second half of joy and purpose. It includes crafting a purpose statement that will be your compass as you explore new contexts in which to thrive and seek out new relationships, both of which will help you live out who God has made you to be. Be prepared to step way out of your comfort zone, as so many women you'll meet in this book have done.

While these four stages are sequential, the process of living them out is not. Life and personal growth rarely proceed in a linear fashion, which means that navigating each of the four stages requires some back-and-forth. For example, as you work through the second and third stages of Get Free and Get Called, you may need to revisit the first stage of Get Clear to clarify who you are and who you are not. At every stage, you will need to be curious about your life, willing to learn new things, and prepared to make adjustments. In our own lives as well as with the women we coach, we've discovered that the key to navigating this transformational process well is to embrace three essential practices.

THREE ESSENTIAL PRACTICES

Transformation at midlife is not only possible, but it's also an exciting adventure—one that has the potential to change every area of your life and all of your relationships. Once you decide to embrace change rather than resist it, your halftime will be increasingly filled with joyful anticipation of where your journey will lead.

We've found that a cycle of three practices is especially helpful in the process of learning to embrace change. The cycle is pray, act, adjust.

Committing to these practices will help you navigate the four transformational stages by inviting God into your journey, creating forward momentum, and embracing new learning and relationships. As you continue to pray, act, and adjust, you'll be drawn deeper into the transformation process and begin to experience positive change unfolding in your life.

Pray

To pray is to have a conversation in which you share your emotions, concerns, and questions with the God who knows and loves you. We say that prayer is the foundation for change because change requires living with an uncomfortable amount of uncertainty and unknowns. You are headed into uncharted territories and will not have all the answers you want as quickly as you want them. To navigate that well, you will need awareness, insight, and wisdom beyond your own. And you'll need the steady comfort and reassurance of knowing that God is with you each step of the way.

Begin by making prayer an intentional daily practice. Although it's always good to pray spontaneously and on the go, setting aside a specific time and place helps to make prayer an intentional part of your change process. You might start with just five to ten minutes at the beginning or end of your day. Use your time with God to share any emotions, concerns, or questions you have about your halftime experience and the changes you face. Ask for what you need—guidance, wisdom, practical help, comfort, a next step. Then listen—deeply.

Beyond that, there are any number of additional ways to incorporate prayer into your journey. You might read a devotional, write out your prayers in a journal, or use a daily prayer app. Use this book as a prompt to pray before you read each chapter and work through the exercises. You can also use the daily routines of life as prompts for prayer—pray on your commute, pray as you prepare meals, pray while walking the dog or working out. If you are able to read the book in community with others, pray before you meet and pray with one another when you are together.

The words you use when you pray do not matter. However, having an open, curious, willing heart to explore new possibilities does matter. Why? Because God is endlessly creative and probably has plans for you that you never could have dreamed up on your own. If you are looking for God's best for your life, you don't want to miss out on that because you were unwilling to be open to new possibilities. He is ready to take your hand and walk this path with you.

Giving your journey to God in prayer with consistency will not only give you the guidance and reassurance you need, prayer will also give you confidence to take action as you trust God to lead you through this process.

Act

Taking action is required throughout the entire four-stage process. To act means to take a step forward. It might be a simple step, such as recording your thoughts in a journal as you work through a self-awareness exercise. Or it might be a riskier step, such as contacting people in a ministry or organization you are interested in, or even joining that ministry or organization for a short time to try a new role that's outside of your comfort zone. We stress taking action because you will never be able to merely *think* your way into moving forward; true change requires you to *act* your way forward. To take one step, and then another and another.

The challenge is that taking action is often hard, especially when you feel depleted or confused. What can make it even harder is the expectation that if you follow God's best plan for your life, everything should be easy—all the doors will open, and you simply have to walk through them. However, one look at the life of the apostle Paul in the New Testament proves how misguided this expectation is.

In pursuing his God-given calling and his second-half journey, the apostle Paul was stoned, dragged through the streets, left for dead, shipwrecked, and imprisoned. And yet, at no point did Paul allow his difficult circumstances to keep him from taking action and pursuing his calling. In fact, when Paul encouraged his protégé, Timothy, to live out his God-given calling, he also warned him that there would be difficult times ahead. "Anyone who wants to live all out for Christ is in for a lot of trouble," he wrote. "There's no getting around it. . . . But don't let it faze you" (2 Timothy 3:12-14, MSG).

If Paul is our example of what it means to take action, you may be tempted to put the book down at this point. Understandable. While we hope the actions you take will be easy and flow seamlessly for you, you would be the first if that's the case. Instead, we invite you to hold on to the promise that, regardless of your circumstances, God will make known to you the path of life and fill you with joy in his presence (Psalm 16:11). This means you should expect that taking action will be hard, and that this is normal. God is at work in your hard times as he makes known to you the path of life for your second half.

Adjust

Taking a step forward doesn't mean that every step will be an instant or obvious winner or turn out as you hoped. In fact, if you expect change to be a "one and done" process, you're setting yourself up for frustration and disappointment. If anything, change is more like a "many and never done" process. That's why learning to adjust may be the most critical skill to develop as you navigate your halftime season.

To adjust means you are able and willing to pivot, to be nimble, flexible, and open to new ideas, people, and places. Being able to adjust is what enables you to consider alternatives and discern the best way forward rather than simply jumping to the next thing that presents itself. Adjusting might be as simple as letting go of plans that have been on the calendar for months or as complex as letting go of a relationship or a position in order to make room for something new.

Learning to adjust well—without giving in to discouragement, despair, and self-pity—not only keeps our mind and heart open to the new thing God may be doing, it also increases our ability to learn and grow along the way. A willingness to adjust, to flex with changing circumstances, brings joy, hope, and energy back into our lives.

> "My life had become safe and small, yet my heart longed for something big and bold. God's plan for my life was changing."
>
> *Marsha Gordon, PhD, Halftime Institute certified coach*

Honing our adjustment skills also enables us to approach this season with a sense of adventure and curiosity rather than resistance and dread. That's why a key aspect of adjusting is learning to normalize failure. Getting caught up in perfectionism or expecting every action to succeed is a surefire way to kill a sense of adventure and curiosity.

Normalizing failure is an acknowledgment that things will not work out perfectly all the time—and that's okay. We encourage our clients and friends to focus on actions rather than outcomes.

Did you take an action to move forward? That's a success, even if it didn't turn out as you hoped. In that sense, there is no failure at halftime as long as you're willing to keep trying. As you pray, act, and adjust throughout the four transformational stages, keep your focus on progress, not perfection. It is simply a matter of time until you find your sweet spot.

THE CHOICE TO CHANGE

Embracing change began for me with the yell-praying session on my bedroom floor: "Finish what you started in me, God. Your love is eternal—don't quit on me now." The actions I took next and the difficult choices I made to move forward ultimately led me to a one-on-one coaching program at the Halftime Institute. One of the first things my coach told me was that God's plans for me were bigger and better than anything I could dream up on my own. And he was right. It took hard work to get clear on who I am, to get free from what was holding me back, to embrace my calling as a coach, and to get going by pursuing the work I love. Although the changes I experienced happened over a decade, my entire life was transformed through this process.

My coach also told me that the choice to change was mine alone to make. So I want to challenge you with the same challenge he gave to me: "The first step to changing your life is realizing that you are responsible for your life. You're responsible for where you are now and for where you will go next."

It's a choice that faces every woman at halftime: *Am I willing to take responsibility for my life? Am I willing to take one step and then another? Am I willing to change?* And the God-given path to transformation that follows will be as unique as the woman who makes that choice.

- "I now know there will never be another person on earth who has the same purpose or calling as I do. Using my strengths of compassion, encouragement, discernment, wisdom, positivity, empathy, and adaptability, I believe the impossible is now possible—that I can help others to be set free from lies and anchored in love and joy."
  —*KP LoveJoy, founder of LoveJoyCO*

- "Being who God calls me to be now and doing what matters most has been my transformational journey. Before, I was simply busy—head down and plowing through life. God showed up to help me get clear. What I yearned for most was to be present for Wayne and our kids. Now I have arranged my life so I can be present for them while also growing as a coach and being open to serving others."
  —*Nancy Lopez, leadership and career transition coach*

- "In my second-half reinvention, the Lord turned my focus toward the future instead of only looking back at what I had once loved doing. I am now aware of opportunities that are a part of God's new path for me. Instead of searching desperately for what the plan is, I let it unfold in my life."
  —*Loretta Leffin, anxiety mentor*

If you're willing to make the choice that these women and so many others have made, we promise that a more joyous and abundant life is available to you. It's a promise we can make with confidence because we have witnessed transformation in the lives of hundreds of women just like you who have made that choice. It is incredible to see what happens in women's lives when God shows up.

Our prayer is that you will experience renewed joy, hope, and purpose as you trust God and take one step forward and then another. You are entering deep heart and soul work that really can transform the trajectory of your second half. We celebrate and honor your courage as you embark on this journey with us.

ESSENTIAL PRACTICES

PRAY

Share. As you consider embracing change in your life, what worries, unease, or fears do you have? What excitement, anticipation for the future, and pops of joy are filling your heart right now? God already knows your concerns and is waiting for you to open your heart to him.

Ask. What wisdom, help, or resources do you most need from God to embrace change this next season? Ask him to open new windows in your heart and doors of opportunity in your life to welcome this transformation.

Listen. Quiet your mind and heart for the next several minutes to listen for the gentle, comforting voice of the One who knows you thoroughly and loves you unconditionally.

ACT

Journal your initial thoughts in response to the questions that follow. This action will help you begin to get clear on your current reality, explore your intentions, and open your mind to possibilities for your future.

- What prompted you to begin your halftime journey?

- What do you hope might be different because of your half-time journey?

- If there were no limits and you could be and do anything, who would you be, and what would you do?

ADJUST

What adjustment do you want to make—just one at this point—to take a step forward?

GET

Part 1

CLEAR

SHAYNE

Sitting on the edge of my bed, I throw my laptop away from me with disdain and fume, "Carolyn wants me to do *what*?"

Glaring at my computer dangling precariously off the edge of the bed, I have the urge to finish it off, kick it to its death on the hardwood floor.

Letting out a deep sigh, I begrudgingly retrieve the laptop and reread her questions: "If there were no obstacles, what do you want your life to look like? What is the dream for your life?"

My emotions—self-pity, depression, loss—threaten to overwhelm me. *My dream?*

All I feel is rage.

I am a cliché. A girl interrupted. A traumatic event disrupted my life, relationships, and career, and I cannot get past it. For years, I have been searching for—*something*. A job? But not just any job. In the past, I worked as an author, a speaker, an advocate, and an educator. I traveled as a writer, reporting on what life is like for women and girls living in unthinkable economic and domestic circumstances, working for change for women and girls globally. I want that kind of meaning back in my life now. I *need* purpose. Something I can be all-in on that is far removed from this painful season and something—*anything*—that is outside of the four walls of my house and my now-grown children's lives.

The previous several years had brought intense darkness. I was abandoned by lifelong friends in an hour of need; I was treated poorly in a professional environment by Christian women I trusted deeply yet who betrayed and attacked me. I was the personification of that person lying on the road to Jericho in desperate need, wounded and bleeding. Yet, friends, family, colleagues, and faith leaders walked around and over me without mercy. Where was my Good Samaritan?

It had happened years earlier, but I was still struggling. *Will I never get past those experiences? Why am I so stuck?*

As I stare at Carolyn's questions on my laptop, tears slowly fall down my cheeks. I feel more alone and alienated than ever. *Are there women out there who can answer this question? Who have a dream for their lives?*

Carolyn, my Halftime Institute coach, thinks so. But I feel like a failure even in terms of how I ended up having coaching sessions with her. She is an *executive* coach. My husband is the one who discovered the Halftime Institute and signed himself up when he unwound his firm and was looking for his next thing. But he ended up finding his next thing before he did any of the coaching sessions. After years of listening to me complain and cry about how I have no life, he donated his sessions to me.

I reluctantly agreed to try the coaching because I am tired of feeling the way I feel. I am stalled, and I have no idea what to do. I have gotten nothing but "no" down every path. I pray, cry, and beg God to use me again. I am embarrassed and humiliated that I seem to be of no use to anyone. I send résumés, I volunteer. But I do not trust myself. I feel I have made a series of bad choices, even though I made them based on sincere prayer, faith, and trust. I feel foolish.

I feel as though God doesn't care either. So many things had come and gone in my life by the time I reached fifty, but my relationship with God had always been my one constant. He had never left me, and this relationship is so hard to put into words. He was so close to me during hard times, the only one who saw, who knew, and who loved without judgment. Yet, today, I find myself utterly devastated by God's silence. *Is he leaving me too?*

I am an extrovert, a list checker, an organizer worker bee. I love to work. *Why is there nothing for me? Why did I choose to stay home with my children?* I feel so stupid. I should have been working this whole time so I would have something of my own: a career, a body of work, a better degree.

I understand most people who do career coaching are men. Men who have been successful influencers and leaders. Men who have created great wealth and resources. I am none of these things. I feel pathetic. One day, a well-intentioned friend asked why I was so depressed. I moaned like a little child and said, "My kids are gone! I feel like I've been left behind." I just sat sobbing.

It is abundantly clear that what I am doing or not doing is not working. I can stay in this place of discouragement and self-pity, or I can take risks, show up, and push through this barrier.

Deep breath. *Pull it together.*

I did my Halftime homework as instructed. I tried and felt foolish in trying, and I answered Carolyn's questions. As simple as they were, her questions were difficult and painful to answer, requiring me to search my heart and life to find what I authentically believed about God, the world, and myself at midlife.

For twelve months, Carolyn and I did this often-painful back-and-forth. We had monthly coaching calls with homework and readings in between. During these times, Carolyn spoke truth into my heart and life. One day, she tried to assure me, saying, "So many women at midlife feel exactly the way you do. Stuck. The good news is you are just beginning this journey. A midlife journey is more like growing corn than popping it. It takes time. It is like a mystery unfolding."

After listening to more of my tearful self-pity, she said, "The bad news is, discouragement is very normal. However, here's a word of encouragement for you: Transformative growth takes time. Sometimes, when we begin a new phase of life, there is an initial decline before growth."

2

TURN YOUR
DREAMER BACK ON

*What astounded her more than anything was that she felt
as though a haze had lifted recently, and she could see in a way
she hadn't been able to before. . . . She was ready to take some
risks and start walking in the direction of her dreams.*

LOUANN BRIZENDINE, MD, *The Female Brain*

SHAYNE

The candles flickered gently in the evening breeze as I sat with
a friend on her screened-in porch. We were chatting about our
children leaving for college after a busy summer with everyone
unexpectedly home because of the COVID-19 pandemic. Now
that restrictions were lifting and her two kids were heading back
to college, the reality of empty nesting was hitting her hard.

"I don't know what to do with myself," she said. "I suppose I
have things that can keep me busy, but . . ." Her voice trailed off,
and then she pointed to her temple. "It's empty inside."

"What do you dream about doing?" I asked. "What's your
dream life scenario?"

"Pfft," she scoffed. "I have no idea."

WHAT HAPPENED TO YOUR DREAMS?

When you were just a little girl, some caring person may have asked, "Who do you want to be when you grow up? What do you dream about doing with your life?" And chances are, you had no shortage of answers. *I want to be a teacher. I want to fly to the moon. I want to work with horses. I want to be president. I want to live in a castle. I want to be a doctor. I want to have lots of kids and live in the country.* Dreaming was as natural to you as breathing.

And yet, if another caring person were to ask you those same two questions today, the answers probably wouldn't come so easily. Like my friend on the porch, when asked about your dreams, you may even draw a complete blank. Why is that? What happened between childhood and today? What happened to your dreams? Why is your dreamer turned off?

"Some of the obstacles that held me back from a successful midlife transition were insecurity and doubt. I was always putting my dreams on a shelf for another time in life."

Tracey Lynn Russell, host of The Heart of the Story *podcast*

It may be that you actually accomplished the dreams you had early in life. Perhaps you founded and ran a successful organization, had a fulfilling career, or raised children and are proud of the people they have become. Your dreamer is turned off because you feel you have nothing left to dream.

Perhaps the dreams you had in young adulthood were snuffed out when life dealt harshly with you, and you know all too well the pain of broken dreams. Now you struggle to dream again because it feels dangerous, especially if it seems like no one believes in you, supports you, or even sees you. Your dreamer is turned off because you're afraid to hope.

It could be that the demands of life make it seem impossible to dream right now. You're navigating difficult circumstances or relationships. When you look to a future with no children at home, a marriage that needs work, or an unwanted career change, all you feel is fear, anxiety, shame, or emptiness. Your dreamer is turned off because you feel overwhelmed by life.

Or perhaps the idea that you could have a new dream for this season of life seems almost absurd—out of line after your years of sacrifice for family, a career, or both. Isn't dreaming reserved for younger women? Your dreamer is turned off because you believe your season for dreaming is long gone.

Whatever the reasons may be, the dreams that came so easily to most of us in the first half of life now elude us. And yet, if we want to live a life of joy and purpose in our second half, we have to turn our dreamer back on.

So what exactly is your dreamer, and what do we mean by dreams? Your dreamer is simply that part of you that is able and willing to aspire to new and better things. When your dreamer is turned on, you feel free to imagine new possibilities, new ways of living, and new relationships. In fact, you not only feel free to imagine these things, you feel excited about the adventure of making your dreams a reality.

When we speak of dreams for women at halftime, we are speaking of both your *being* and your *doing*. Dreams are aspirations, longings, glimpses of whatever you want to be true in your life. More specifically, dreams include whatever it is that would make your second half most meaningful—anything from the kind of person you want to be, to how you want to spend your time and where you want to live. Dreams hold the key to God's best

WHAT WOMEN SAY ABOUT THEIR STRUGGLE TO DREAM

Many of the women we coach find it difficult to turn their dreamer back on. Perhaps you will resonate with some of their struggles.

- "When the kids left home and I stopped working, I thought, *What is my value? What is my purpose?* For several years, I searched for answers through Scripture and prayer. I didn't find any answers to my questions."

- "Even successful corporate women have been doing life with constraints, especially as mothers. As career women, we also need to learn how to dream without constraints. We are so used to optimizing under constraints that we're not sure what to do when there are no more constraints. It feels scary."

- "I don't think most husbands understand the fear of dreaming. In our culture, men have always been taught that the sky is the limit, but that is not the experience for most women."

- "I can imagine bigger things for my life, but I also get stuck. As women, we do turn off our dreamer. We do not dream as freely as men do because we do not feel we have permission in the midst of all the caretaking we do."

- "I had success in my career before I had a family. Then I had all the significance I could ever want when I was a full-time mother. Now that my kids are on their own, I'm not sure what success or significance means, much less what it means to dream."

- "When I think of midlife, the emotions that come to mind are confusion, insecurity, and discouragement. I doubt I will ever get a chance to try something new."

for you—the person he created you to be and the work he has uniquely prepared you to do.

We believe that it is possible to turn your dreamer back on and that you can have new dreams for your life. We believe God isn't finished with you yet. And we believe that everything you've learned, experienced, and overcome in the first half of life has given you a unique treasure trove to draw on so your next season really can be filled with joy and purpose.

MINE YOUR TREASURES

CAROLYN

Turning your dreamer back on begins by mining your treasures— the gifts, resources, wisdom, and so much more that are hidden within your life experiences and the desires God has placed in your heart. If you're like many women at halftime, your initial reaction might be to think you have no treasures. In fact, you may feel you are at a deficit, that you are less than, or that you have been left behind and no longer have much to offer. And yet nothing could be further from the truth. Whether or not you realize it, your life—past, present, and future—is rich with buried treasures. On the pages that follow, we will walk you through a series of exercises to help you mine those treasures, but first we want to acknowledge a few things about the emotions that may arise in the process and provide some guidelines for navigating this process well.

"Halftime started for me when I left a job that was limiting my potential. It was a time of conflicting emotions: peace and stress, joy and sadness."

Michelle Kilbourne, PhD

Transformational change is emotionally challenging. You might experience feelings that range from ambivalence to excitement, from fear to hope, from grief to delight. It is vitally important to honor all of these emotions. In fact, we invite you to welcome them, sit with them, write them down, and listen to what they have to say. However, when the emotions are negative ones, it can be easy to fall into one of the two temptations—to avoid them altogether, or to get stuck by focusing only on what is wrong or what has been lost.

It is difficult to tap into your dreamer and your hopes for the future when you're either actively suppressing or feeling overcome by emotions. While it's important to honor and acknowledge all the emotions, it's also important to not allow negative ones to dominate your outlook. The purpose of mining your treasures is to flip the narrative by focusing primarily on what is good and life-giving in your past, present, and future. With the apostle Paul, we invite you to fix your thoughts on "whatever is true, whatever is honorable, whatever is just, whatever is pure, whatever is lovely, whatever is commendable" (Philippians 4:8, ESV).

As you work through the exercises that follow, when a negative emotion or memory arises, notice it but then continue with the exercise. In short, notice and move on. It's a practice drawn from a model called Appreciative Inquiry (AI), and I use it often in my coaching. To appreciate is to recognize the best in people and circumstances and to affirm strengths, successes, and potentials. To inquire is to explore, discover, ask questions, and be open to new possibilities. So to approach your life with a sense of appreciative inquiry is to appreciate, value, explore, and discover your unique story and to find the treasures that are keys to your future and this process of change.

Here are some guidelines to help you get the most out of the exercises in this chapter and in the chapters that follow.

- Set aside at least thirty minutes for quiet reflection, ideally in a tranquil and beautiful place. Or if you're able, plan to take a day or more for a silent retreat so you can have an extended time to pray and reflect.

- Write down your responses to the exercises in a journal. In addition to helping you to reflect more deeply, documenting your responses provides vital information that you will continue to reflect on and refer back to over time. In fact, you'll be asked to review what you've written for additional insights at the end of each of the four stages.

- Work through the exercises with a trusted friend, spiritual advisor, coach, or small group. Sharing your story and allowing others to affirm it not only provides much-needed companionship, it can also provide valuable insights and direction for your next season.

Now it's time to mine your treasures—past, present, and future. In the process, we hope you will begin to discover renewed gratitude, joy, and hope.

Gratitude: Riches from Your Past

In a recent coaching session, the woman I was working with began to cry. "I feel completely unequipped to turn my dreamer back on," she said. "I have no idea where or how to start."

When I hear cries for help like this, I invite women to begin with gratitude, mining the riches from their past. Beginning with gratitude brings up positive memories and powerful emotions that often point to future dreams. In that sense, the first step in turning your dreamer back on is something like excavating for treasure because the clues to unraveling the mystery of your second half are often buried somewhere in your first half.

Begin by identifying five things you are most grateful for in your past. Consider your relationships, circumstances, and opportunities. Also reflect on any treasures that were hidden in your hardships, mistakes, or failures, especially what you learned or how your character was shaped. Note any graces, gifts, miracles, or mercies you received. If you find it helpful, reflect on your life by decades. What are you most grateful for from the first decade of your life, your teens, your twenties, and so on?

Here are some examples of what other women have found when mining the riches of the past:

- "I am thankful for the corporate job in which I excelled. While I was a busy single mom, we always had food on the table and a solid roof over our heads."

- "I can now say I appreciate my parents bringing me to the United States at an early age. Even though I looked and felt different from everyone else, I gained empathy and compassion for all races and cultures."

- "I am grateful that God never left me, even as my abusive husband finally walked out the door. I am grateful to be alive, to be wiser, and for the chance to make different choices for my second half of life."

- "I'm so grateful to have raised my children well and launched them into the world."

Once you've identified the five things for which you are most grateful, use the following questions to unpack each one.

- What role did you play in this event or experience?

- What role did God play?

- What relationships, if any, made a positive contribution to this event or experience?

- What made the environment a life-giving one?

- What activities did you enjoy most?

- How did this event or experience make a difference in your life or in the lives of others?

Here is how the single mom with the corporate job used the questions to unpack one of the five things for which she was most grateful.

- What role did you play in this event or experience? *The role for which I am most grateful in life is that of just being a mom. While I worked hard and excelled in business, that was never the most important part of my life. Coming home to my two children was the experience for which I am most grateful.*

- What role did God play? *God was my everything, our everything. There were days I didn't know how I would make it; the busyness of being a single mom made life a blur. But somehow, I knew that God was always there.*

- What relationships, if any, made a positive contribution to this event or experience? *My parents were a godsend during this time. My mom has since passed away, and I still remember her as my best friend. If I had a late meeting, which was often, both Mom and Dad would pick up the kids after school. I have no idea how I would have handled being a single mom without their support.*

- What made the environment a life-giving one? *When I think about the environment during this time, I think of Mom and Dad's house first. While I loved going to my own home, it also reminded me how much I needed to do to keep everything going. Our house was so busy, but Mom and Dad's house felt calm. It was a small, cozy home with a beautiful garden. Life felt simpler there. I felt at peace, like I could really relax.*

- What activities did you enjoy most? *I loved being a soccer mom. Seriously! I was a soccer mom, basketball mom, field hockey mom, swim mom. I spent so much of my life sitting on the sidelines cheering for my kids. It was never a waste of time for me; I loved every moment of their sports activities.*

- How did this experience make a difference in your life or in the lives of others? *Being a mom was everything to me—the most significant accomplishment in my life. It is hard to imagine anything more important than watching my two girls become beautiful, self-sufficient women. I am crying as I write this because, while everything feels scary and confusing right now, I know I did the best I could to raise my children well.*

The power of gratitude can help you remember what brought you joy—the people, events, and experiences that helped you feel fully alive. And these riches from your past may be clues to your future. For the single mom, although her role as mother to small children was ending, her dreams for the future were tied to slowing down and creating a calmer and more intentional life. While she wanted to continue to excel in her second half, she also knew she wanted to take on less responsibility. Remembering her parents' home became a clue that helped her identify the kind of environment she wanted to create in her second half of life.

Joy: Gems from Your Present

Dreams are an expression of what brings us joy. We dream of a relationship because we feel nothing could make us happier than to be a part of this person's life. We dream of an experience because we can't imagine any more meaningful way to spend the next decade than contributing to this cause or living out this passion. We dream of an event because the very thought of it coming true brings happy tears to our eyes.

Even if you don't yet feel like you have a clue about what your dreams might be, you likely do have clues about what brings you joy. By joy, we mean any experience, however small, that makes you smile, gives you energy, or makes you feel more alive. When you mine the treasures of the present, you focus on noticing what is right in front of you; what brings even a flicker of joy to your heart. You collect gems that may eventually point to your dreams—and those dreams may be closer than you think.

Begin by focusing on your day-to-day roles, activities, relationships, and environment. Your task is to notice and document whenever you feel a pop of joy, a spark of energy, or a sense of coming alive. And by document, we mean write it down by taking literal notes—in a journal, on a pad of paper, or even on your smartphone—ideally, right in the moment.

- What brings a smile to your face?

- What makes your heart come alive?

- Who are you with when you feel joy?

- What does your environment look like?

In addition to noticing what brings you joy, it's also important to note anything that diminishes your delight in life. Write down the things that steal your joy, sap your energy, or make you feel less alive.

Make it a daily habit to notice your joy givers and joy takers, write them down, and then move on with your day. If you forget to do so in the moment, you can still do a joy review at the end of the day. Reflect on each part of your day—morning, afternoon, and evening—and write down whatever brought you joy or took joy from you. In the process, you'll develop a new level of self-awareness as you move through your day noticing what does and does not bring a flicker of joy to your heart.

Your daily experiences of joy are clues to your future. Once you've collected five to seven days' worth of joy documentation, do a weekly review of what you've written. Look for any patterns that emerge or threads that connect one experience to another. For example:

- What roles consistently bring joy or take joy?

- What activities consistently bring joy or take joy?

- What environments consistently bring joy or take joy?

- What relationships consistently bring joy or take joy?

Keep up the daily habit of documenting joy and the weekly habit of reflecting on any patterns you can identify. All of them are treasured gems that can move you closer to your dreams.

Hope: Gold for Your Future

God knew you would be in this place in life, and he knows your next best steps. He knows and treasures the dreams of your heart, and that changes everything. Mining for gold in your future is essential for learning to dream again.

Begin by imagining yourself in a scene many years in the future, your final season of life. In your lap is a photo album packed with snapshots from your second half. As you flip through the pages, what images do you hope to see of yourself and others? What roles, activities, environments, and relationships do you hope will be pictured there? The goal is to set the scene of your future and your second season with no limitations. Be as wild and creative as you want to be. Allow yourself to be an audacious dreamer, maybe even a rebellious dreamer. Gather the images for your second half as if no one and nothing were saying no to you.

Here are three options you can choose from to help you collect your future snapshots.

Imagine your snapshots and write them down. What snapshots do you want to see in your future? Whose faces do you hope to see smiling back at you? What relationships are mended, restored, or flourishing? What environments are you in? What activities and roles are you are engaged in? What images would make you feel that your second half had been meaningful, rich, and rewarding? Write down everything you imagine in your journal.

Create a Pinterest board. Start with images rather than words by creating a Pinterest board. Create separate sections for each of the four categories: roles, activities, environments, and relationships. For each category, pin images that spark joy, creativity, and curiosity in you. Pull together images that depict what you value most for your future and the dreams you have for yourself.

Take photos on your phone. Another way to gather images is to take photos on your phone as you go about your day. Snap pictures of things you want to be part of your life in your next season. Again, focus on capturing images of the roles, activities, environments, and relationships that spark your dreamer. Collect all the images you capture into a "Dream" album on your phone.

Whichever option you choose, take as long as you need to gather your images—a week, a month, or even longer if needed. Then set aside time to review, reflect, and make sense of what you have assembled. As you reflect on the words you've written or the images you've gathered, what stands out most to you? Are there consistent themes in your images? What surprises you? What scares you? What creates a pop of joy in you? Write down all your observations in your journal. All the treasures you excavate are clues to help you dream big dreams for your second half.

DARE TO DREAM

To dream is to risk, and that can be scary. It sparks resistance in our hearts and minds because it feels vulnerable. And yet, as uncomfortable as it may be to consider dreaming again, your willingness to even consider taking a risk is actually a sign of strength and

A DREAM OF WIDE-OPEN SPACES

SHAYNE

One night, I had a dream. In it, I am walking over a barren hill. I have never been here before, but I am not lost. I am alone in a colorless scene when I hear a voice call my name. It is the voice of someone who knows me and loves me. Emphatically and with great anticipation, the voice says, "Shayne, it is drawing near! It is coming! It is ancient!" I eagerly peer over the rise of the mountain where the voice is coming from and I see it: a deep well appears in front of me.

I believe dreams are messengers, and I awaken wondering about the message of this dream. It reminds me of an Old Testament story about wells, specifically, a passage that tells the story of the wells that Abraham dug. At that time, wells indicated ownership and rights to the land. In this story, Philistines had maliciously filled all the wells with dirt and debris, clogging them up and cutting off the very supply of life (Genesis 26:17-24).

As the story goes, when Abraham's son Isaac moves back to the Valley of Gerar, he commits to redigging the wells of his father. When he reclaims the first well, it once again provides fresh water. But then the shepherds of Gerar quarrel with Isaac's men, so Isaac names this well Esek, which means "quarrel." Isaac moves on. His servants redig a second well and again find life-giving water. Another fight ensues over this one, so Isaac names the second well Sitnah, which means "accusation" or "hatred."

When Isaac and his men dig a third well, they encounter no resistance, and so Isaac names the well Rehoboth, which means "wide-open spaces." He says, "Now God has given us plenty of space to spread out in the land" (Genesis 26:22, MSG). That night, God appears to Isaac and says, "I am the God of Abraham your father; don't fear a thing because I'm with you" (Genesis 26:24, MSG).

This story ignites my spiritual imagination and I now see my soul as something like one of Abraham's wells. The challenges of life have filled my soul with the dirt and debris of broken relationships, quarrels, and resistance. Yet there is a well that contains no resistance or fear, one that is given by God. It is life-giving, and it is filled with purpose, joy, and hope. There is a wide-open space I long for, a space where my soul can be free, and I can become who I am meant to be.

courage. As author Brené Brown explains it, "Yes, we are totally exposed when we are vulnerable. Yes, we are in the torture chamber that we call uncertainty. And, yes, we're taking a huge emotional risk when we allow ourselves to be vulnerable. But there's no equation where taking risks, braving uncertainty, and opening ourselves up to emotional exposure equals weakness."[1]

We can't dream without risking what feels like failure, and yet, we believe that there is no such thing as failure in this process, only learning. If you are willing to take a risk, you can learn what works for your next season and what needs to remain in your past. This is one step closer to your dreams.

Turning your dreamer back on is the starting point for your halftime journey because every part of the process that follows—Get Clear, Get Free, Get Called, Get Going—builds on it. As you get clear on who you are, your dreamer begins to stir. When you get free from whatever may be holding you back, your dreamer takes a deep breath. When you get called by God and believe he has specific things for you to do, your dreamer is energized. And when you get going and take some risks, your dreamer is fully engaged and back on. It is a process, it is *this* process, and we invite you to take the risk to dream again.

ESSENTIAL PRACTICES

PRAY

Share. What emotions, concerns, or questions arise as you mine the treasures of your past, present, and future? As you consider taking the risk to dream again? Share your heart with God.

Ask. What do you need right now? For example, guidance, practical help, comfort, courage? Ask God to provide for you.

Listen. Sit in silence for a few moments, listening for anything God might whisper to your heart.

ACT

- Complete the three exercises described in "Mine Your Treasures" (pages 33–40).

- Identify one action you can take in response to what you learned or discovered from the three "Mine Your Treasures" exercises. Remember, to act is simply to take a step forward. For now, focus on something small you can complete within the next day or two. Write it in your journal.

- Journal your responses to the following questions.

  » What comes to mind when you envision "wide-open spaces" for your next season?

  » What roles, activities, environments, and relationships would help you to feel free to be all God made you to be?

ADJUST

As a reminder, to adjust is to be nimble, flexible, and open to new ideas, people, and places. To practice adjusting is to consider alternatives and discern the best way forward. It may mean starting something new or letting go of something old. Based on what you've learned from taking action, what adjustments do you want to make? Consider any adjustments in thought, speech, or behavior that could help you move forward. Write them in your journal.

RECLAIM YOUR TRUE SELF

The first half of life, my identity was in raising my children,
my work, and supporting my husband's career.
Halftime started for me when the children left home,
and I was no longer working. I felt uncertainty and loss of identity.

ELIZABETH DEAN, *Mothers of Preschoolers (MOPs) lead mentor mom*

Before having children, Camille thrived as a bank vice president and area manager who oversaw thirteen branches. When children came along, she poured her heart and skills into being a stay-at-home mom, school board member, and church leader. Throughout her child-raising years, she had been so busy running here, going there, and taking care of everyone else that she didn't have much time to think about her own life.

When her daughter left home for college and her son was eagerly filling out college applications, life beyond the nesting years looked lonely.

"It was like, now what?" Camille recalls. "I felt an emptiness. What's going to happen now? What am I going to do? I had been on the board of the children's school, and that had been my identity. I was *her mom*; I was *his mom*. But who would I be now?"

IDENTITY LOST

When you first meet someone, how do you introduce yourself? Who do you say you are? If, like Camille, your identity has been tied to raising children, you might introduce yourself as Jack's mom at a high school basketball game or Rachel's mom as you proudly watch a dance recital. If you have built your identity as an entrepreneur or corporate executive, you might introduce yourself by describing your work or naming your organization. Or it could be that your identity is tied to another person, to status symbols or accomplishments, or even to traumas such as a death or divorce. While all of these things are important, none of them are what truly make up your identity.

Your identity is who you are at your very core, even when you are not doing anything at all. Author and psychotherapist Ruthellen Josselson describes identity this way:

> Identity is the ultimate act of creativity—it is what we make of ourselves. In forming and sustaining our identity, we build a bridge between who we feel ourselves to be internally and who we are recognized as being by our social world. When we have a secure sense of our identity, we take ourselves for granted as being who we are. We feel at home in ourselves and in our world, and have an inner experience of coherence and purpose.[1]

In the first half of life, our identity tends to shift, attaching itself to significant people and responsibilities. Many mothers build their identities around their children, whether they work outside the home, inside the home, or both. Women also build their identities around a career, a husband, extended family, or aging parents. While all of these people and responsibilities are important, too many of us overidentify with those things and lose touch with who we are without them. When our relationships and responsibilities change, we wonder, "Who am I now?"

One of the most heart-wrenching challenges of midlife is having our identities stripped away. Even if we realized this season or this job would come to an end, our hearts are unprepared for the sense of loss and grief when it actually does. Who are we now, at the heart level, without the title, the child at home, or the person who left us?

Reclaiming your true self is an essential task of halftime. You will still have significant relationships, and you will still be a contributor—*and* it will look different in your next season of life. Knowing who you are now—not who you once were—is what enables you to make wise choices when moving to your next thing. If you do not know who you truly are and do not have a clear idea of what you want to do with your life, something or someone else will end up making those decisions for you.

Anytime we are in a transition, such as midlife, the temptation is to *do* something—anything—to keep busy. But to enter into your second half well, you first need to figure out who you are. Who you are is primarily a question of being rather than doing. Certainly, who you are and what you do are intricately connected, but they aren't the same. You are a human *being*, not just a human *doing*. When navigating this confusing transitional season, resist the urge to focus on the doing before the being, to jump too quickly to your next thing. To know yourself is to be a protector of your time and purpose. Your path is not just about finding something new to do. Your path is to stop long enough to get clear and reclaim your true self.

IDENTITY FOUND: YOUR EPHESIANS 2:10 CALLING

The biblical foundation for your true self is what we refer to as your Ephesians 2:10 calling:

> We are His workmanship, created in Christ Jesus for good works, which God prepared beforehand so that we would walk in them.[2]

This beautiful promise speaks to both being and doing—who you are (God's workmanship) and what you do (good works). God already knows your best path forward for the good works he has prepared for you to do, and we'll explore that more in chapter 8. But first, let's begin with who you are: God's workmanship.

The Greek word translated "workmanship" is *poiema*, from which we get our English word *poem*. *Poiema* means "something made."[3] In this case, God makes you; you are his creation and his masterpiece. He has skillfully and carefully crafted you in Christ Jesus (2 Corinthians 5:17). A poem is a thing of great beauty and grace. You are unique, a work of art with great value. Even if it doesn't feel like it right now, you are his poem, his beautiful expression. The entire purpose of his work in your life is to conform you into the image of Christ and to express his love, grace, and kindness through you.

"I have found my calling and my identity in allowing God to work through my life as I disciple and lead young moms."

Elizabeth Dean, Mothers of Preschoolers (MOPs) lead mentor mom

This halftime journey is about pursuing not just God's best for you, but God's best expression *of* you—who he created you to be—and then pouring your life into his plans. The Ephesians 2:10

promise is foundational not just because it anchors your identity, but because it means you are not alone and never have been. God knew you from the very beginning and called you his workmanship, his beautiful creation.

Take a moment to allow that truth to sink in. Your true self is surrounded by love. Even now, God is wrapping his arms around you and telling you that he is crazy in love with you. He delights in you. You are his masterpiece, his beautiful work of art. He is not shocked by your challenges, and nothing can ever separate you from your Creator. He is big enough to handle anything in your life because he already knows your true identity. You have the freedom to take risks because you can trust him with who he says you are. You are loved. You are complete. You are a work of art, valued and cherished. The spiritual foundation for reclaiming your true self begins with love and grace.

IDENTITY FOUNDATIONS

You build on the spiritual foundation of your identity by exploring who you are and who you are not, at least not anymore. This foundation encompasses all that God has given you and all that you have experienced up to this moment, both positive and negative. Externally, your identity has been shaped by fulfilling experiences, relationships, and blessings, as well as losses, pain, and tragedies. Internally, your identity includes your unique talents and strengths, the superpowers that God has given you from birth. Upon inviting God into your life, you were also given spiritual gifts for equipping the church. You may have had moments when you felt the flow of God's Spirit giving you wisdom, warning you of dangers ahead, or leading you to help others. All of these unique and wonderful gifts make you who you are.

To help you begin to reclaim your identity foundations, it's essential to be clear about your strengths, your spiritual gifts, and who you are and are not.

Identify Your Strengths

Gallup is an analytics and advice firm that helps leaders and organizations use a strengths-based approach to problem-solving and growth. To help their clients begin to understand and tap into their strengths, Gallup uses an assessment tool developed by psychologist Don Clifton called "CliftonStrengths" or "Gallup Strengths."[4] The assessment divides strengths into thirty-four "talent themes." We've found the assessment to be extremely helpful in coaching women at halftime because the results demonstrate in scientific terms the spiritual truth that all of us are uniquely and wonderfully made. Many women in midlife need to be reminded of this. In fact, according to the assessment, you are so unique that the odds of finding another person with your top five strengths, listed in the same order of intensity, are one in 33 million.[5] Considering that there are thirty-four talents themes, the odds of finding someone exactly like you on this earth is nearly infinitesimal. Knowing your talents and strengths helps you understand yourself at a deeper level: why you are drawn to some roles, activities, environments, and relationships, and not others.

According to Gallup, your strengths begin with your organic

> "I am using my love for my daughters, my relationship-building strengths, and my journey through anxiety to help women from college age to my age learn skills to help them with their anxiety."
>
> *Loretta Leffin, anxiety mentor*

talents, which are defined as naturally recurring patterns of thought, feelings, or behaviors that can work for you or others. These talents are part of who you are and how you are uniquely wired. Your talents can be developed into strengths when you invest time, knowledge, and practice in building them. Think about strength training at a gym—you may have the potential to develop strong muscles, but until you actually lift weights, your muscles will remain weak. When you commit to developing your natural talents into strengths, these become your superpowers, areas in which you naturally excel that are rooted in who you are at your core.[6]

In assessing talents, Gallup looks for a sense of excellence, feelings of flow, yearning, and satisfaction. While excellence means being exceptionally good at something, "flow" describes something that comes easily to you, where you feel you are in the zone of life. You may recall the classic movie *Chariots of Fire*, based on the story of Olympic runner Eric Liddell. Liddell felt called to the mission field as his life purpose, but he also recognized his natural talent. "I believe God made me for a purpose," Liddell said, "but He also made me fast. And when I run, I feel His pleasure."[7] That experience of divine pleasure is also connected to yearnings, another part of your talent mix. Yearnings are what you are naturally drawn to. You tap into yearnings when you feel you are in exactly the right place doing exactly the right things.

Gallup captures all of these components in a simple equation:

$$\text{Talent} \times \text{Investment} = \text{Strength}$$

In other words, your talent, multiplied by the time you invest in practicing your skills and building your knowledge, equals your strength, which is the "ability to provide consistently near-perfect performance."[8] The feeling of excellence, being in the zone of life, a yearning in your heart for something, and the satisfaction you experience when using your strengths all contribute to what makes you feel alive.

To simplify things, Gallup groups its thirty-four talent themes into four domains: relationship building, influencing, strategic thinking, and executing.[9] Think of these domains as on-ramps you can use to begin rediscovering your strengths. We all have strengths and talents in all areas, if we choose to build them, but some will come more naturally to you than others.

Relationship building. Women who are skilled at relationship building have a knack for working with others and building strong teams. Talents in this domain range from being a natural includer (noticing when someone feels left out and bringing them in), to being a gatherer (having a positive energy and an engaging spirit that brings people together). You may be that empathetic soul who is a trusted friend—one who reaches out to others, is sensitive to their feelings, and is forgiving. Your talents may range from bringing harmony in relationships to recognizing the unique gifts and potential in others.

When Camille began exploring her strengths, her top relationship-building skill turned out to be empathy—she could sense other people's feelings by imagining herself in their situations. Camille also had the uncanny ability to sense unvoiced needs and concerns, and she experienced glimpses of excellence and God's pleasure when she reached out to help address those needs. Camille felt in the flow of life by naturally knowing just what to say to those in need. It came easily to her. She yearned to help others and received great satisfaction in return.

When have you sensed glimpses of excellence, flow, yearning, or satisfaction in your relationships with others? Write down everything that comes to mind. Your relationship-building talents may be clues to your strengths.

Influencing. Influencing talents describe those who know how to motivate others, advocate for themselves and their teams, and generally have no problem meeting new people. Those who rate high in influencing talent themes range from expressive communicators to those who love to maximize the work of teams and individuals.

Think of that individual who loves to bring people together and makes the team a better, more motivated group by just being there. One of my colleagues, Brenda O'Donnell, is a great example of someone with influencing talents. Brenda is a natural at taking charge of a situation, speaking up for others, and motivating individuals and groups. She loves meeting new people, breaking the ice, and making relational connections with others. She feels at her best at social events and often makes it a goal to say hello to everyone in attendance. These interactions bring her tremendous energy.

When have you sensed glimpses of excellence, flow, yearning, and satisfaction through influencing? Focus on times when you motivated others, had a positive influence on an individual or group, or helped someone maximize their potential. Write down everything that comes to mind, no matter how small. These, too, are clues to your strengths.

Strategic thinking. Strategic-thinking talents describe those who love to analyze and absorb information. Their talents range from being detail oriented and able to think analytically, to being fascinated by creative ideas. Strategic thinkers can often sense patterns and see a way forward that others miss. These are the visionaries in our midst.

Camille discovered that one of her greatest talents, learning,

ASSESS YOUR STRENGTHS

Psychologist Don Clifton, who created the CliftonStrengths assessment, was extremely interested in human development and behavior, particularly in how human beings excel. Once when he went to a library and asked to see the resources focused on what is right rather than wrong with people, the librarian told him there was no such section in the library. So Clifton set out to create it.[10]

We encourage all the women we coach to take the CliftonStrengths assessment. It features 177 questions that measure thirty-four talents in four domains. Completing the assessment takes thirty to fifty minutes. To help you answer instinctively, the assessment allows about twenty seconds to respond to each question. The short amount of time is designed to mimic the quick decisions often required in real-life decision-making.[11] To learn more about the CliftonStrengths assessment, Google "CliftonStrengths assessment" or visit www.gallup.com.

was in this domain. She said if she learned something in a day, that day was a success. Camille realized that she also had the talent of quickly discerning relevant patterns and issues to find the best path forward. Her natural strategic-thinking gifts later became important to deciding the next best steps for her second half.

When have you sensed glimpses of excellence, flow, yearning, and satisfaction in how you process information? Write down what you know about how you process and absorb information, including any examples that come to mind. These are clues to how God has uniquely wired you.

Executing. Executing talents are characteristic of those who know how to make things happen. Those with executing talents are often achievers who can take an idea and make it come to life. They have natural talents for organizing events, problem-solving, and consistently accomplishing tasks, regardless of challenges.

Within the domain of executing, Camille found her primary talent to be belief. The talent of belief is what enables a person to act from their passions and core values. Camille is passionate about the cause of education, even though she felt a shift in her role in her second half.

When have you sensed glimpses of excellence, flow, yearning, and satisfaction by getting things done? Write down what comes naturally to you in the domain of executing. These sweet spots are clues to your strengths.

Identify Your Spiritual Gifts

While strengths describe your natural talents and areas of excellence, spiritual gifts are given to everyone who is a follower of Jesus Christ. The apostle Paul describes spiritual gifts as a "manifestation of the Spirit for the common good" (1 Corinthians 12:7, ESV), and states their purpose as "building up the body of Christ" (Ephesians 4:12, ESV). Every believer has at least one spiritual gift, and it's not uncommon to have multiple gifts. God not only wants you to be aware of your spiritual gifts, he wants you to use these gifts and grow in them each day. Remember, you are God's workmanship, a masterpiece created by, through, and for Jesus Christ.

Scripture identifies eighteen spiritual gifts. As you read through the list, consider which gifts you might have or want to learn more about.

1. *Administration:* the ability to plan, organize, and/or provide leadership to a church or ministry (1 Corinthians 12:28; Romans 12:8)

2. *Apostleship:* the gift of individuals who go out into the world to preach the gospel, such as missionaries and church planters (Ephesians 4:11-12; Acts 13:6-12)

3. *Discernment:* the ability to bring wisdom to situations and to individuals who wish to follow God's teachings (1 Corinthians 12:10)

4. *Evangelism:* the gift of teaching the message of salvation and spiritual truths (Ephesians 4:11-12)

5. *Exhortation:* a gift that goes beyond teaching by offering support and encouragement, a spiritual cheerleader (Romans 12:7-8)

6. *Faith:* unwavering belief in God and in Scripture (1 Corinthians 12:9)

7. *Giving:* a gift that enables a person to give generously and with pleasure and purpose (Romans 12:8)

8. *Healing:* the ability to heal and restore others, physically and otherwise (James 5:13-15)

9. *Helping:* the gift of supporting another member of the body of Christ so that they are free to use their gifts (1 Corinthians 12:28)

10. *Hospitality:* the ability to welcome others into a home or church with warmth and a serving spirit (1 Peter 4:9-10)

11. *Knowledge:* a gift expressed in a desire to study the Bible and the ability to analyze Scriptures and retain information for the furthering of the Kingdom of God (1 Corinthians 12:8)

12. *Leadership:* the ability to motivate others in the body of Christ to achieve Kingdom objectives; often seen in pastors, teachers, evangelists, and lay leaders (Romans 12:8)

13. *Mercy:* the gift of sensitivity to the needs and suffering of others (Matthew 5:7)

14. *Prophecy:* the ability to speak into the lives of others on behalf of God (1 Corinthians 14:1)

15. *Serving:* a gift similar to helping in which individuals have a heart to serve the church and other believers in practical ways (Romans 12:7-17)

16. *Speaking in tongues:* the ability to speak a spiritual language while filled with the Holy Spirit (1 Corinthians 12–14)

17. *Teaching:* the ability to clearly teach the Bible, doctrine, and church history to others (Exodus 4:12; 1 Peter 4:11)

18. *Wisdom:* the ability to see clearly in complex situations and arrive at solutions (1 Corinthians 12:8)[12]

Although the Bible doesn't provide a set formula for identifying spiritual gifts, there are four steps that have helped many women we coach to discover their gifts. We encourage everyone we coach to pray, serve, consult others, and take an assessment.

Pray. As with all things, and especially in this halftime process, the first step is to start with prayer. Ask God for guidance and discernment. Rely on this promise: "Ask and it will be given to you; seek and you will find; knock and the door will be opened to you" (Matthew 7:7, NIV).

Serve. Begin serving at your church or volunteering with a charitable organization. Author and pastor Charles Stanley says, "Probably the best way to discover your gift is to serve in a variety of ministry situations. When you find the area that suits your gift, you will know it."[13]

Wonder if you have the gift of mercy? Look for a prison or hospital or hospice ministry. Think hospitality is right up your alley? Offer to be a greeter at your church or to host new member coffees or receptions for visiting teachers and missionaries. There is no limit on how or where God can use your spiritual gifts. Begin serving and discover where your sweet spot is.

Consult others. Ask the Christian friends who know you best which spiritual gifts they see in you. These conversations can bear much fruit and can also be incredibly encouraging and affirming. In addition, you may wish to consult a ministry leader, pastor, elder, or small group leader who knows you well and who has experience in helping others identify and use their spiritual gifts. Many churches also offer classes for those wishing to go deeper into identifying and utilizing their spiritual gifts.

Take an assessment. There are multiple books and online resources, some of them free, that provide assessments to help you identify your spiritual gifts.[14] We find that these tools are most effective when used in combination with the previous steps— praying, serving, and consulting others. Continue to seek God's guidance and invite trusted friends and mentors into the process as you identify your spiritual gifts.

Through coaching, getting free from what held her back, trying out some paths forward, and finally, pressing into her true identity, Camille was able to understand herself at a deeper level. Camille's primary spiritual gift turned out to be giving. She is an excellent steward of her resources and always on the lookout for an opportunity to help others. In addition, she is a joyful giver, and this trait became crucial to her second-half purpose. Camille also has the gift of discernment as she can easily distinguish between truth and lies. Her challenge is to use this gift and trust her God-given instincts in this area. Camille also ranked high in the gift of faith. Here you can see where spiritual gifts and strengths begin to work together. Her gift of faith resonated with her strength of connectedness. Camille has a confident faith that there is a greater purpose and she is connected to her benevolent Creator.

Identify Who You Are and Who You Are Not

Your purpose in your second half will become more apparent as you identify who you are and who you are not in four primary areas: roles, activities, environments, and relationships. You've already done some thinking about these areas in connection with turning your dreamer back on. Now we invite you to take another step by identifying who you are and who you are not in each of these areas. After reading through the descriptions of each area, use the charts on the following pages to reflect on who you are and who you are not.

Roles. Roles are the parts you play in different seasons of your life. For example, you may have had roles such as wife, mother, friend, executive, or entrepreneur. Roles also change within a family, organization, or ministry. For example, you may start out as a participant in a MOPs group and then move into the role of being a lead mentor in the group. Identifying the role(s) you want for your second half will be especially important in preparation for part 4, Get Going.

Who I Am Not	Who I Am
• What roles have you lost or no longer fit?	• In what roles do you thrive or feel energized? • What roles allow you to use your strengths and spiritual gifts?

Activities. Activities are something you do as part of your daily work and your purpose. Activities can be for fun, such as a social interest, or they can be part of your vocation, such as a business involvement. An activity might be structured as part of a formal ministry, or it could be something you enjoy doing on your own, such as walking or bicycling. Activities represent the *doing* part of your life.

Who I Am Not	Who I Am
• What activities have you lost? • What activities no longer interest you?	• What activities energize you or make you feel in the zone? • What activities give you a glimpse of excellence or help you feel you are making a contribution?

Environments. Environments are the places and conditions that surround us.[15] Think about where you have felt most alive in your life, the contexts in which you can best thrive and grow. For example, some women might thrive in a busy urban setting, whereas others might feel at their best in nature. Some may feel celebrated in a large group of people with lots of activity and action, while others prefer a peaceful, quiet place. However, environments aren't limited to geographic locations. Environments also include the conditions of the place you are in, such as the beauty or feeling of safety you experience there. As you think about the environments you want to be in, try to recall the kinds of places you've been when you felt most empowered and free to be yourself. In your memory, look around and describe the environment.

Who I Am Not	Who I Am
• What environments have you lost access to? • What environments deplete you?	• What environments do you yearn to be in? • What environments energize you or bring you joy?

Relationships. Relationships are the support system you have around a common purpose, background, or interest. Relationships include family, friends, work colleagues, and ministry or volunteer connections. In helping those in transition, Halftime Institute founder Bob Buford asks people about their relational "islands of health and strength"—in other words, those who build you up, add energy to your life, and help you to move forward.

Who I Am Not	Who I Am
• What relationships have you lost? • What relationships have changed? • What relationships bring you down or make you feel less than your true self?	• What relationships do you long for? • What relationships bring you joy and peace? • In what relationships do you feel free to be yourself?

We've just covered a great deal of content about the foundations of identity. While it may feel like a lot to absorb and process, it is more than worth the investment to do so. When you are clear on your strengths, spiritual gifts, and who you are and are not, you can build a strong and firm foundation for your second half.

BEWARE OF IDENTITY THIEVES

In the process of reclaiming your true self, there will be some obstacles you'll have to overcome. We call these identity thieves, and the three most critical ones to be aware of actually reside within you: comparison, attachments, and guilt. The good news is that when you're aware of these identity thieves, you can confront them and send them packing.

Comparison

Someone has wisely observed, "Comparison is the thief of joy." It can also be the thief of identity, as Camille learned when she was in a halftime coaching program with four other women. "I would size them up," she says, "and all I could think was, 'Oh my goodness, I will never measure up.' One woman was sending Bibles to China, and another had a big job in the financial world. All I had been doing in recent years was making lunches and attending sporting events."

Comparison robbed Camille of joy and led to discouragement. She used to say, "I am going to flunk halftime." It wasn't until she began to explore her strengths and spiritual gifts that she was able to take her eyes off what other people were doing and focus on what she was uniquely gifted and called to do. Then, as if magnified by love, one word on her strengths list stood out: learner.

There it was—her foundational strength, the one that resonated most with her true self. It was a pop of joy that helped her to set comparison aside. She embraced the promise that God's dreams for her were better than anything she could think up on her own. She would become a student of her own life so she could move forward into a renewed purpose.

Don't let comparison steal your joy. Don't let it become a distraction that focuses your energy on others. Don't miss what is right inside of you. Confront the identity thief of comparison to reclaim your true self.

In what ways, if any, are you comparing yourself to others? How does this keep you from moving forward?

Attachments

Attachments are anything you cling to that prevents you from moving forward. At halftime, this includes continuing in patterns of thought and behavior that may have served you well at one point but no longer do, such as doing what you have always done just because you've always done it. Anything you hold on to that no longer works for you or that actually prevents you from moving forward is an attachment.

Attachments often become most apparent when you're beginning to discover your strengths and looking forward to a new purpose. That's when the past may call to you, as it did to Camille. "I was grieving the loss of being involved in my kids' daily lives at school when the school asked me to step in as chairman of the board," she recalls. "I felt drawn to it but also conflicted. This had been my identity for so long—his mom, her mom. I knew I would always be their mom, but things were changing as my babies left for college. Even so, it would have been easy to say yes.

"I had been praying and asking God to help me take my next steps when it just hit me. Continuing to serve at the kids' school was not what God wanted me to do. I had been in leadership at the bank, my church, and the kids' school, but maybe God was calling me to leadership in a different way." It was time for Camille to say goodbye to what no longer fit so she could keep moving forward.

What are your attachments—things you might be clinging to that no longer fit or align with your identity? How do these attachments keep you from moving forward?

Guilt

Guilt is another identity thief that can keep you from finding your true self. Particularly the guilt of disappointing others.

Other people may have their own ideas of who you should and should not be. When you begin to make changes, especially letting go of things that no longer fit, you may have to say no and disappoint these people. Those who respect boundaries and personal growth will accept your decisions, but others may not. In fact, they may try to guilt or pressure you into not making changes. It is crucial to recognize these tactics for what they are— toxic influences.

You do not have to feel guilty for wanting to dream new dreams, try new things, or make positive changes to move forward. If you find yourself thinking things like *I'm afraid to take this step because it will disappoint someone* or *I can't let this go because it will create a hardship for someone*, your identity is in the clutches of guilt.

Protect your heart. If there are people in your life who are pressuring you to be someone you are not, you may need to distance yourself from them if you can or set a boundary to keep them from intruding on this area of your life. Give yourself a break from judgmental people and your own guilt over disappointing them.

In what ways, if any, might guilt about disappointing others be keeping you from moving forward?

YOUR EPHESIANS 2:10 CALLING AWAITS

As Camille identified her strengths and gifts—empathy, learning, giving, and encouraging others—she was able to get clear about who she was at her core. Believing in the connectedness of their shared purpose, Camille and her husband ultimately started a foundation that enabled them to invest time and resources in causes they believe in. Embracing her faith and her passion for learning led her to also take on the role of being a Bible teacher to women in her community. She now expresses the heart of her God-given identity this way: "Be the ears to listen, the heart to feel, the tongue to encourage."

Most importantly, Camille learned the most powerful lesson of this process—that she was loved, accepted, and whole just as she was. She was already pleasing to God because her identity was firmly rooted in Christ. As she considers new opportunities, her guiding words are *grace* and *trust*. Anything she decides to do from this point on will be based on the knowledge that she is God's creation. "We are His workmanship, created in Christ Jesus for good works, which God prepared beforehand so that we would walk in them" (Ephesians 2:10, NASB).

Your Ephesians 2:10 calling is waiting for you. It has been created just for you by the Poet who delights in you and loves you, even on your most challenging, horrible day. The next step is yours to take. Building on your dreams and what you are discovering about your true self, it is time to begin composing a new verse for your next season.

ESSENTIAL PRACTICES

PRAY

Share. Talk with God about any new perspectives you have about your true self. What strengths do you recognize? What feelings are you aware of as you begin to pursue your Ephesians 2:10 calling?

Ask. What wisdom do you need right now? What resources can help? Who might God bring to you to provide insight and encouragement on your journey?

Listen. Ask God to give you insights as you walk this new path. Then sit in silence for a few moments, inviting him to speak to you.

ACT

- Complete the exercises described in "Identity Foundations" (pages 52–63). Note that some of these exercises, such as identifying your spiritual gifts, may require an extended period of time.

- Journal your responses to the questions about comparison, attachment, and guilt at the end of each section in "Beware of Identity Thieves" (pages 64–67).

ADJUST

Based on what you've learned from taking action, what adjustments do you want to make? Consider any adjustments in thought, speech, or behavior that could help you move forward.

For example, you might identify adjustments in the way you view your strengths and spiritual gifts, or note any conversations you may need to have with others about your boundaries and needs as you reclaim your true self. Write the adjustments in your journal.

IDENTIFY YOUR VALUES

How have I changed between the first half of life
and the second half? I speak up more. I acquiesce less.
I don't care about going along as much.

MICHELLE KILBOURNE, PHD

For thirty years, Marnie Nair had both lived in and served at-risk communities. With a doctorate in language and literacy from Harvard, she devoted her life to teens, whom she loved as if they were her own children. She also spent time volunteering in Cambodia and Rwanda and worked to expand educational opportunities for Syrian refugee children in Jordan and Lebanon. By the time Marnie came to us for coaching, we might have thought that her life was already full and satisfying—until she shared her story.

"On the verge of turning fifty, I was suddenly slammed with the realization that I hated my life," Marnie says. "I remember the exact moment when it dawned on me that I had become a person I did not recognize. Instead of a fun-loving, happy-go-lucky, free spirit, I had become a person who worked night and day. And when I was not working, I had zero energy left to live life."

Ten years prior, Marnie had become founding director of a small charter school in San Diego that served newly arrived refugee students. It was a passion project, and she loved the school and the students. Yet the demanding nature of the work also left her depleted. Marnie worked nonstop doing tasks that were not life-giving. Year after year, she told herself a time would come when things would settle down and then she would begin to enjoy her work. But the school kept growing, and there was always a new challenge.

As a lifelong entrepreneur, working hard was nothing new to Marnie, but now she felt sucked dry. No matter what she tried, Marnie could not find her enthusiasm and joy. "I had always felt a midlife crisis was a joke," she says, "an excuse for a middle-aged man to buy a red sports car and leave his wife for a younger model. Yet, there I was, in the middle of my inability to get it together—and it was no joke."

Marnie had planned to be at the school until she retired, and she had no backup plan. But one day, she just knew she was done. She had no desire to work a single day more than she had to, and she set about preparing for and implementing a smooth transition of leadership. Then Marnie quit—not just her job but life as she knew it. She moved across the country and decided to take a sabbatical year to recover.

"When I left my life in San Diego, I felt very uncertain about most things," she says, "but one thing was absolutely clear to me. I had created an organization with values built around everyone thriving—except me. To ensure that others were in life-giving roles, I had given myself a role that consisted entirely of work that drained my soul."

Marnie knew she was not finished contributing to the world,

but she had no idea what might be next. The only thing she knew was that something inside her needed to shift. She had a vague sense the change required had something to do with her heart rather than her head. Understanding or even acknowledging her feelings had always been a struggle. The idea that being aware of her feelings could help her get clear on her values—what mattered most to her—was a new and daunting idea for Marnie. But listening to her heart, to her soul's longings, was how she would ultimately find her true values.

WHAT ARE VALUES?

Values are qualities of being and doing that define what is most important to you. From love to faith to adventure to humor, values are ideals that motivate you and are essential for you to live from your true self. Your values are realized in your choices—specifically, the choices you make to live them out. According to psychology professor Dr. Steven Hayes, having values requires intentionality. He writes,

> There's no domain, no age, no situation to which values do not contribute. You don't "find" them. You choose them. You have to do the work of exploring and looking and selecting and owning.[1]

Because values are qualities that inspire us, Hayes also points out that they can never be fully achieved, only embraced and demonstrated—and doing so is what puts us on the path to fulfillment.

Just as what we believe about God will be evident in our lives, our values will be evident in our actions. Our values give us direction and drive our decisions and behaviors—for better or for worse. When we live out of alignment with what matters most to us, we will eventually lose energy. We may even hit a point when, like Marnie, we realize we hate our lives.

A growing body of research demonstrates that getting clear about values—and especially putting values in writing—significantly increases a person's ability to succeed. We'll guide you through a process to help you get clear on what your values are, but first we want to address an often overlooked yet essential issue.

VALUES AND EMOTIONAL INTELLIGENCE

Whether or not we want to admit it, our emotions can profoundly impact the degree to which we successfully live out our values. According to Daniel Goleman, a pioneer in the field of emotional intelligence, our emotions guide us in facing predicaments and tasks too important to leave to intellect alone—such as danger, painful loss, persisting toward a goal despite frustrations, bonding with a mate, building a family.[2] But emotions can also overwhelm reason and cause values to become unclear. While we can't choose whether or not to have emotions, we can be aware of our feelings and manage our choices and behaviors according to what matters most to us—which is where emotional intelligence comes in. Before we address that, however, we first need to understand something about how emotions sometimes bypass our values. Here's a scenario that demonstrates that.

Imagine you have a value of relational connectedness. One morning a call comes in on your cell phone. The caller ID indicates it is the person you are avoiding, the one you don't want to speak with (we all have them). Your brain reacts. How do you feel? Do you honor your values and take the call or let it go to voice mail?

The call is what's referred to as an event, and you can't help but have emotions tied to it. A recent study found that we have more than 6,000 thoughts a day, and every one of those thoughts has an emotion connected to it.[3]

So how does your brain process all these thoughts and emotions?

It turns out you have two distinct parts of your brain—the thinking brain and the emotional brain. The thinking part of your brain is the prefrontal cortex. It manages logic, decisions, and behavior. Also known as the executive center, the prefrontal cortex is responsible for what we usually associate with the brain—making rational decisions. However, at the back of the brain is something called the amygdala. This is the emotional part of your brain. Before any thoughts are processed by the prefrontal cortex, they pass through the amygdala. In other words, the brain processes events emotionally before it processes them rationally. When you encounter an event your amygdala considers an imminent threat, it can bypass rational thought by responding instinctively to keep you safe. It's what's called an "amygdala hijack."

"At midlife, I was anxious, nervous, and touchy. I wanted my sense of humor back. I wanted to find my center and walk in alignment with my own values, not a corporation's values statement. At work, I was slowly stepping back and avoided raising my hand for new assignments. I was yearning for quiet moments and time in nature. The whisper got louder. 'It is time.'"

Virginia Sambuco, former customer care executive

Many of us in midlife may remember an anti-narcotics television commercial in which a man holds up an egg and says, "This is your brain." He points to a hot skillet on a stove and says, "This is drugs." He then cracks the egg into the skillet, holds the sizzling egg up to the camera, and says, "This is your brain on drugs." Although emotions certainly don't fry your brain like drugs do, the constant bombardment of those 6,000 daily thoughts and emotions does keep your brain "sizzling" with activity.

When your emotional brain processes events as positive and valuable, this sparks positive emotions, such as feelings of happiness or satisfaction. In this state, you feel creative, engaged, and able to make decisions aligned with your values.

On the other hand, when your emotional brain processes events as negative, this sparks negative emotions, such as worry, frustration, or stress. If the emotional brain interprets the event as a serious threat, it "hijacks" or bypasses the thinking brain, which makes it harder to act in ways that are aligned with your values.

The key to honoring both values and emotions in a healthy way is to develop emotional intelligence (EI). According to Genos International, a research and consulting firm in the EI field, emotional intelligence is the ability to perceive, understand, and reason with our own emotions and the emotions of people around us. When we practice emotional intelligence, we have more productive and positive responses to events, use our emotions to choose what is most important to us, and then live by those desired values.[4]

Perhaps you're beginning to see how your emotions can either empower or hinder your ability to live out your values. When Marnie began her midlife transition, all she knew was that she hated her life. While she had buried her feelings of disappointment, anger, and disillusionment, she couldn't keep these emotions down forever. Event after event in her life broke her down until it was hard for her to even remember what mattered most to her. She

SIX EMOTIONAL INTELLIGENCE COMPETENCIES

Based on research and neuroscience, Genos International identifies six core emotional intelligence competencies. Each competency exists on a continuum that ranges from an "unproductive state" at one end to a "productive state" at the other. In an unproductive state, our cognitive resources are impaired, which means we lose our ability to think and behave creatively and cannot perceive the best way forward. In a productive state, we are aware of and manage our emotions, which enables us to innovate, find solutions, and move forward. The purpose of practicing these core competencies is to become increasingly adept at living in a productive state.

As you read through the descriptions of the six emotional intelligence competencies, try to recall experiences of being in a productive state and being in an unproductive state regarding that competency. For example, when recently have you experienced a productive state of self-awareness? An unproductive state of self-awareness? If you find it helpful, note any insights in your journal.

1. **Self-awareness**: being aware of your emotions and the impact your feelings and moods have on your choices and behaviors. When you are self-aware, you are conscious of how your feelings impact your thinking and quality of life. You are also aware of how your emotions might influence the impact you have on others.

2. **Awareness of others**: noticing and acknowledging others and being sensitive to how others feel. When you are aware of others, you are more empathetic and can view life from others' perspectives. Conversely, when you are unaware of others' feelings, you may be perceived as insensitive or uncaring.

77

3. **Authenticity**: being genuine, saying what you mean, doing what you say you will do. Being authentic means honestly expressing how you feel and what is most important to you, even if it is not the popular opinion.

4. **Emotional reasoning**: using the information in both your feelings and the feelings of others when making decisions. In a productive state, you are expansive and creative; under the amygdala hijack, research shows your ability to make good decisions is limited, and your emotions can shut you down.

5. **Self-management**: managing your own mood and emotions. The good news is that you can manage your moods and emotions and show up with others as resilient rather than temperamental. You can also pay attention to critical self-talk to better manage your life rather than being fueled by negative emotions.

6. **Positive influence**: influencing how others feel by creating a productive and empowering environment rather than showing up as indifferent. When you positively influence others through problem-solving, compassion, and emotional intelligence during stressful situations, you become an encourager and motivator.[5]

had to listen to what her emotions were telling her to get clear on the values she wanted to live in her second half. Whenever your life is out of alignment with your values, your emotions will let you know. Tapping into this God-given gift is emotional intelligence.

IDENTIFY YOUR VALUES

One way to begin thinking about your values is to consider what you love most in your life. For example, the roles, activities, environments, and relationships that bring you joy and inspire you. The key is to name what you really do care about, not what you think you should care about. Another way to get clues about your values is to pay attention to what moves you emotionally when you read a book or watch a movie. Note what you resonate with in the story or which character inspires you. Or you might make a list of people you admire and jot down their characteristics. Those characteristics are often excellent clues to your values. Other good clues might come from a favorite Bible verse, or from any personal or family mottoes you may have. For example, "Be kind every time," "I can do hard things," or "Just keep swimming."

Keep your clues in mind as you complete the following exercise, which is designed to give you a jump start in identifying what matters most to you.

- On pages 80–81 is a starter list of "100 Value Words." Review the list and circle all the words that resonate with you. If you think of other words that aren't on the list, write them down.

- Next, review your circled words and narrow your choices down to the five words that most reflect your values. The key is to be true to what matters most to you. For instance, you might value the fruits of the Spirit, such as love, joy, peace, and patience, but the more specific value is safe and loving relationships. Be brave and authentic in circling the values that matter most to you.

- Write your five values in the left column of the chart on page 83. Or, if you'd prefer, re-create the chart in your journal and complete the activity there.

100 VALUE WORDS

Accomplishment	Flair
Accuracy	Focus
Action	Forgiveness
Adaptability	Formality
Adventure	Freedom
Authenticity	Friendship
Beauty	Fun
Candor	Gentleness
Challenge	Gratitude
Cleanliness	Hard work
Collaboration	Harmony
Commitment	Honesty
Community	Hope
Competence	Humor
Comradery	Improvement
Cooperation	Inclusion
Creativity	Independence
Decisiveness	Informality
Democracy	Innovation
Discipline	Integrity
Discovery	Intensity
Diversity	Involvement
Elegance	Joy
Equality	Justice
Excellence	Kindness
Fairness	Knowledge
Faith	Leadership
Fame	Learning
Family	Love
Financial security	Loyalty

Nonviolence	Simplicity
Nurture	Skill
Order	Spontaneity
Patriotism	Stability
Peace	Standardization
Perfection	Status
Personal growth	Strategy
Power	Success
Practicality	Teamwork
Preservation	Timeliness
Privacy	Tradition
Prosperity	Tranquility
Recognition	Trust
Results	Truth
Risk	Unity
Romance	Variety
Safety	Vulnerability
Self-control	Wealth
Service	Winning
Significance	Wisdom

- In the right column of the chart on page 82, write the feelings you associate with each word. For example, the word *discovery* might generate feelings of being alive or excited. Don't over-think it; simply write down whatever comes to mind.

- Briefly review what you've written and then rank your five words in order of importance. Use a 1 to 5 scale, with 1 being your most important value, 2 your second-most important value, and so on. Write the numbers next to each word and then circle your most important value on the chart.

My Top Five Value Words	How These Value Words Make Me Feel

Once you've completed the chart, use your journal to reflect on the following questions.

- As you worked through this exercise, what feelings, if any, surprised you? Why did they surprise you?

- In what ways is your life already in alignment with the values you identified? In what ways is it out of alignment with the values you identified?

This exercise is just a starting point. Consider your chart a working document, one you will likely update as you continue to get clear on what matters most to you. If you are working through the book with a coach, counselor, spiritual advisor, friend, or small group, be sure to process your values with them. There's no substitute for the support of others who understand you, truly see you, and love you unconditionally. Invite their feedback and insights for your path forward.

PRACTICE SELF-MANAGEMENT, SELF-AWARENESS, AND AUTHENTICITY

Once you've identified your top five values, the next important step is to not only practice those values but to do so with emotional intelligence. To start, you'll focus on three of the six emotional intelligence competencies—self-management, self-awareness, and authenticity. These three competencies reflect the *being* side of who you are. Developing them is foundational work because values only make a difference in your life if you practice them, and emotional intelligence is what keeps you from getting stuck in the process.

It's also important to acknowledge that your relationship with God is the ultimate foundation for both values and emotional intelligence, especially when you're struggling to make a connection between the two. Take it from Marnie.

Failing to live by her true values is what had left Marnie feeling hopelessly depleted and stuck. Although she had always had a clear sense of what her values were, they existed theoretically rather than practically, and it took some time for her to sort things out.

"I remember going to work every day and complaining to my husband that I was adding to the degradation of society. My values no longer aligned with those of my workplace. I was paid well and had achieved a pretty good status at work, but I was miserable. I can't remember how many times I wrote my resignation letter."

Debra Dean, PhD, *organizational leadership*

As part of determining what mattered most in her second half, Marnie was challenged to set aside her mornings to rest and be with God. As it turned out, this spiritual discipline— an expression of her value of faith—was what ultimately enabled Marnie to get unstuck. It wasn't until she was able to quiet herself in God's presence that she was in a state of mind to practice competencies such as self-management, self-awareness, and authenticity.

"This time continues to be sacred to me, the most cherished part of my day," she says. "Each morning, I rise early and make myself a delicious cappuccino. I sit in the coziest corner of my sofa and read my Bible. I talk to God. I think. Setting aside this space has become a sacred ritual that has made room for God to work and speak."

As you read through the descriptions of the three emotional intelligence competencies that follow and consider what it might mean for you to practice them, also consider your own state of mind in this season. If you are preoccupied by stress and worry much of the time, it will be difficult to think straight, much less be open to new possibilities. In order to practice your values with emotional intelligence, you will need to first quiet your heart and mind. Consistent time with God can help calm your worried thoughts so you can live out the values that are most important to you at this stage of life.

Practice Self-Management

Self-management required Marnie to be aware of how she managed her own mood and emotions. When she began to reflect on how she had treated herself over the previous ten years, she made some important discoveries.

"I woke up dreading each day, and it showed up in my self-talk," Marnie says. "No matter how early I got up, my first thought of the day was something like, 'Marnie, you are such a loser. You are already behind on your day.' No wonder I dreaded each day! Who wants to wake up to that message? And by the end of the day, my self-talk wasn't any better: 'Marnie, you did not get a single thing done today.'"

And yet, the facts were that Marnie felt this way while successfully running a school with a multimillion-dollar budget, a staff in the double digits, and a student body in the hundreds. She knew her self-talk didn't make sense—she was busy from morning to night—yet at the end of every day, she couldn't figure out where the time had gone. She felt defeated and overwhelmed by a task list that was never complete. And her negative self-talk and emotions persisted into her sabbatical year.

In coaching, Marnie was challenged to write a list of what mattered most to her now. Not surprisingly, her list did not include managing budgets, hiring, fund-raising, disciplinary actions, or nonstop meetings. Instead, her list included spending time with friends and family and enjoying meals and times together. That's when it dawned on her that there was a disconnect between her responsibilities and her values. At the school, she had often fallen behind on administrative tasks (her job responsibilities) because she was talking to a student or a struggling teacher (her values). As a result, she was actually beating herself up for living her authentic values.

In her sabbatical year, she still tended to discount how she chose to spend her days, even though she consistently made choices to spend time doing things that were in keeping with her most deeply held value, which was close relationships. People mattered most to her. Once she understood that she needed to self-manage when it came to her mood and emotions, she had a light-bulb moment. To focus on what was truly important to her, Marnie could self-manage by prioritizing her time and tasks in accordance with her values. Then she could let go of self-condemnation, shame, and feeling like a failure.

It's been said that the most difficult person to manage is yourself. The challenge of self-management is to take responsibility for your own moods and emotions, including negative self-talk. The invitation is to be kind to yourself rather than your own worst critic.

What comes to mind when you reflect on both your values and your self-management? In what ways does your self-management align with your values and not align with your values? In what ways, if any, might you have become your own worst critic?

Practice Self-Awareness

Practicing self-awareness required Marnie to be more aware of how her feelings and moods impacted her choices and quality of life. That's when she realized she had spent ten years trying to be someone she simply was not.

After her sabbatical year, Marnie found a job with a consulting project related to her interests in education. However, it wasn't long until that familiar pattern of negative self-talk began to creep into her mind again. There was a sales aspect to her position that she felt ill-suited to. While others on the team were thriving, Marnie felt frustrated and inadequate. There seemed to be a lack of strategic vision, and she felt dishonest promoting the product. A negative loop began to play in her head: *Why is everyone else able to sell this product? What is wrong with me that I have a problem but no one else does? Everyone else is better at this than I am.*

Once again, Marnie was trying to be someone she wasn't and found herself in a role that did not reflect her true identity. This time, however, she practiced self-awareness by noticing how her emotions were impacting her. As she pondered her feelings, bathed her mind in Scripture, and prayed, a new self-awareness emerged. It was a new version of self-talk that took the form of God speaking to her.

Marnie, these people have seen your résumé. They hired you, knowing your background. You are not a salesperson—so what? They already have people whose strength is promoting products. But you recognize something important that the others either cannot see or are unwilling to address. You have something to offer that would substantively improve this product. Why are you trying to be like someone else when there is no one else with your strengths on the team? Your insight is important. The worst they can do is fire you—and so what? You are not enjoying this as things stand. You're in a trial period before committing long-term, which means you have an opportunity to be different. Why don't you just be yourself and see what happens?

Instead of falling back into the negative pattern of casting aside her values, feelings, and needs, Marnie made a courageous decision. As she excitedly put it, "I decided that I'm just going to be Marnie!"

With this new insight, Marnie switched her focus from her negative feelings to developing constructive suggestions for the problems that had troubled her. At the next corporate meeting, she proposed a strategic plan and laid out a framework for moving forward. The CEO was so pleased that within a week, she proposed changing Marnie's position to focus on strategic planning and project development, both of which were much more suited to her interests and skills. This allowed her to contribute to the project in ways that felt both authentic and meaningful. Her willingness to practice self-awareness enabled her to change her quality of life by allowing her to be herself at work.

When you are clear about who you are at your core and the values that really matter to you, you are empowered to make choices that honor your values. You practice self-awareness by taking note of the emotions you experience as you live, or fail to live, in alignment with your values. Self-awareness becomes emotional intelligence when, as Marnie did, you make choices that honor who you are and what matters most to you.

In your current context, what triggers negative or unproductive emotions that limit your ability to live in alignment with your values? What sparks positive emotions that help you to live in alignment with your values? What do your emotions reveal about what is most important to you?

Practice Authenticity

Authenticity was a natural outcome of Marnie's decision to just be herself. She gave herself permission to honestly express what she felt and what was most important to her, even though it initially felt like a risk. And that's when the floodgates of authenticity opened wide. Although she had routinely struggled to complete coaching exercises focused on her emotions and values, her difficulties disappeared almost instantly when she chose to simply be herself. Now Marnie could easily identify the moments in her life that had been most meaningful. It was as if she suddenly knew what her values were and what she most enjoyed. Here is what she identified as being most authentic to who she was.

My most meaningful moments
- Having dinner parties at my home
- Traveling with my parents
- Watching students present work
- Listening to teachers I have coached brainstorm new ways to teach

My most enjoyable activities
- Traveling in the developing world and meeting the locals
- Cooking
- Kayaking
- Hanging out with longtime friends

My values
- Laughter
- Friendship
- Hospitality
- Honesty
- Excellence

You might wonder, as Marnie did, "Where are the entre-preneurial, type A personality values and activities on this list?" Although she was driven to pursue excellence, Marnie realized that she was also somewhat different from the typical hard-driving entrepreneur. And that was okay. She felt confident in who she was and in knowing God still had good work for her to do.

Even more critical, Marnie realized that what mattered most to her was a closer walk with God, as evidenced by the time she committed each morning to spending with him. "When I think about the impact of my halftime journey, I feel most excited about the fact that my walk with Jesus is so sweet these days," she says. "Also, I have identified my core values, and I have a much clearer sense of the Marnie Jesus uniquely created me to be. Jesus is going to continue to allow me to participate in his story of redemption."

On the other side of these shifts, Marnie, who considers her-self primarily a thinker, can now feel the emotional impact of her values. She understands that she thrives on challenges, enjoys excellence, and considers a strategically envisioned venture a thing of beauty. Yet the most significant impact of practicing self-management, self-awareness, and authenticity has been finding what she truly values most, which then translates to her second-half actions. Marnie summarizes what matters most this way:

"Follow Jesus. Pursue excellence. Prioritize relationships. Relish creation." Practicing her values with authenticity enabled her to live into her purpose.

In what ways, if any, are you trying to be someone you are not? What positive outcomes might result if you allow yourself to just be you?

WHAT MATTERS MOST

The realization that it's possible to live in alignment with what matters most is one of the most freeing discoveries for many of the women we coach. Identifying values, being aware of the feelings attached to them, and then practicing these values with emotional intelligence is a crucial step in the midlife journey. Here's how Halftime Institute founder Bob Buford sums up his experience with this part of the journey:

> For me the transition into the afternoon of life was a time
> for reordering my time and my treasure, for reconfiguring
> my values and my vision of what life could be. It repre-
> sented more than a renewal; it was a new beginning. It
> was more than a reality check; it was a fresh and leisurely
> look into the holiest chamber of my own heart, affording
> me, at last, an opportunity to respond to my soul's
> deepest longings.[6]

As you explore the holiest chamber of your own heart and become aware of your soul's longings, your values and your path forward will become clearer. Values are indeed a choice, and they reflect what makes you feel alive and inspired. There is still a lot of life to live in your second half, and taking time to get clear on what matters most gets you that much closer to the life you dream of living. That's how to be unconditionally, unapologetically, and joyfully just *you*. Because you are enough.

ESSENTIAL PRACTICES

PRAY

Share. Talk with the Lord about your five values and the feelings you associate with each value. Tell him what is most important to you and why.

Ask. Seek God's wisdom about the five values you chose. Are they authentic to what's most important to you? Ask for insights about how to practice emotional intelligence as you seek to live in alignment with what matters most to you.

Listen. Quiet your heart and listen attentively for any new perspectives on who you are. Listen for guidance on changes you may need to make to live out your values.

ACT

- Complete the exercises in "Identify Your Values" (pages 78–83).

- Do a little brainstorming to identify three to five ways you can live out your most important value (the one you circled on your chart) in the next twenty-four hours. Pick one idea and follow through on it.

- Journal your responses to the questions about self-management, self-awareness, and authenticity at the end of each section in "Practice Self-Management, Self-Awareness, and Authenticity" (pages 85–91).

- *Optional*: Complete your own version of the three lists Marnie created (pages 89–90) to summarize on one page your most meaningful moments, your most enjoyable activities, and your values.

ADJUST

Based on what you've learned from taking action, what adjustments do you want to make? Consider any adjustments in values, self-management, self-awareness, or authenticity that can help you move forward. Write them in your journal.

GET

Part 2

FREE

SHAYNE

The bustling hallways began to empty as students ducked into their fourth-period classes. Soon it was still as the laughter and hollering, the smiling friends and supportive teachers all disappeared from sight. And there I sat alone at a student desk I may well have sat in as a high school student thirty years earlier. I stared at the clock mounted high on the wall waiting for the thirty-eight-minute class period to go by so I could leave my post as a hall monitor.

A student in baggy sweats and ripped gym shoes shuffled by.

"Can I see your pass?" I asked.

He flashed a pink slip and kept walking.

I was working as a long-term guest teacher, otherwise known as a substitute, at the high school I'd attended in the eighties. During the class periods when no substitute was needed, my job was to relieve a teacher who had hall monitor duty. As I sat staring down the hallway where my student locker had once been, I couldn't help but think that this was likely not the best use of the gifts, talents, and experiences God had given me.

For years, I had tried to find a good fit, a calling. I had written books, spoken internationally, earned a professional certificate in screenwriting from UCLA, and founded a nonprofit writers guild. But I knew in my gut that continuing to run the writers guild was not my life's work. I eventually let it go so I could move on.

Except I didn't really move on to anything else. I left the writers guild, anticipating that doing so would make room in my life for something else, something better. But now almost four years had passed and nothing else had surfaced that seemed to fit my calling. Although I had tried a few things, all my efforts felt random, as if I were throwing spaghetti at the wall and hoping something would stick. But nothing was sticking. I felt like a failure and a has-been, as if both my children at college and the world had left me behind. I was invisible and useless.

I had taken the job at the high school to see if going back to teaching might make sense for me. There was a time in my life when I had loved teaching, loved pouring into students, and loved developing individuals. I thought I'd give it a shot. I did all the work to renew my Illinois teaching credentials because I wanted to have a humble and open heart to however God might want to use me in the world.

And yet here I was, staring down an empty hallway as the minutes ticked by, all the sights and sounds taking me back to the past rather than forward and into what I had hoped might be my future. I suddenly felt discouraged and humiliated. *What am I doing here?* I put my head down on the desk and let out a little moan. *Is this all there is for me?*

This was the last day of the semester. When the final bell rang, I gathered my lunch box, my parka, and my archaic loaner laptop, and walked with confidence toward the exit. As the front doors of the high school closed behind me, I knew I would never return.

5

LEAVE BEHIND FEARS
AND LIMITING BELIEFS

My biggest battle was self-doubt. I hadn't been on an entrepreneurial or corporate trajectory for a long time. When I began to excavate my self-doubt and look at it through a spiritual lens, I saw it for what it was—fear.

CRISTIN PARKER, FAMILY COACH AND CONSULTANT

When Cristin Parker took the CliftonStrengths assessment, she discovered that her top five strengths were Strategic, Futuristic, Connectedness, Relator, and Communication. Cristin was created to be an entrepreneur and a leader. However, she didn't see herself this way. In fact, the thought of being a leader actually paralyzed her. Because she had chosen to leave the corporate world to raise her children, she wasn't sure she would be able to catch up with the latest innovations in her field or still be able to lead a team. She also compared herself to other women her age who appeared to be satisfied with their lives and wished she could be more like them.

"I wanted to be that mom who was great at scrapbooking and had the perfect wreath on my door for every holiday," admitted Cristin. "But the more I worked on my identity and values, the

99

more I realized this was just not me—not who God made me to be. I needed to let go of the details and embrace my gift of seeing the big picture."

Like many women who put their careers on hold to raise children, Cristin was highly educated and skilled. She had a degree in human and organizational development from Vanderbilt and had consulted for a Fortune 500 company. When she read the description of her Strategic strength, she was amazed that it described her perfectly:

> People exceptionally talented in the Strategic theme
> create an alternative way to proceed. Faced with any given
> scenario, they can quickly spot the relevant pattern and
> issues. It is almost a supernatural ability to be able to
> jump into the puzzle and see the patterns. It is not a skill
> you can learn; it is a distinct way of thinking.[1]

Cristin was discovering that she had always been an entrepreneur. She could look back on her life and identify all the ways she had been naturally resourceful. She was the one other people relied on to connect the dots, and to find creative ways to solve problems and meet needs. Even when she worked for traditional companies, she ventured off the beaten path and saw things in a more visionary way than her counterparts did.

As Cristin learned more about herself, her heart began to awaken to a dream of advising "wonderfully dysfunctional" families. She had a vision of creating a strategic process that would help families to unlock their potential at all stages. Her vision included a coaching process to establish a relational health operating system to strengthen the family team by uncovering blind spots, creating a plan together, and connecting in new ways. She had done the hard work of turning her dreamer back on, mining the treasures of her identity, and defining her values. In fact, she had done everything she needed to do to begin living out her second-half dream—except one thing. In order to have the freedom she needed to create this new organization, she first had to address what was holding her back.

COMMON FEARS AND LIMITING BELIEFS

Fears and limiting beliefs are negative thoughts and opinions we hold to be absolute truth. Sometimes they reside in our subconscious, below the surface of our awareness. Other times, they are our conscious thoughts, such as *It's too late to pursue my dreams*. Fears and limiting thoughts might be formed by any number of things: negative past experiences, someone's off-the-cuff comment, cultural messages, social media, or values and beliefs held by our family of origin (or the family we married into). They include any message we buy into that keeps us from moving forward and living into the joy and purpose of our Ephesians 2:10 calling.

When you look to your second half, what do you fear most? "Everything!" was the immediate response of one of our coaching clients. Perhaps you understand how she feels. If so, you're far from alone. Without exception, all the women we've coached have struggled with some combination of fears and limiting beliefs. As we walk through five of the most common ones we've encountered in our coaching work, consider which you relate to most.

"My best years are behind me." The fear that all joy and purpose is lost to the past is by far the number one fear expressed by the women we coach. We heard it from Camille, from Marnie, and from many others. It's a fear shared by both corporate executives

and stay-at-home moms. And many women also suffer from the limiting belief that there is nothing that can be done about it.

"My body will never be the same." Women at midlife have fears related to changes in appearance, menopause, graying hair, weight gain, medical conditions, and more. Commenting on changes in her appearance, one coaching client said, "I feel invisible." Whether they are full-time career women, hybrid working moms, or stay-at-home moms, women often buy in to the limiting belief that they have little to offer in a society obsessed with youth and appearance.

"I am professionally incompetent." Many women who stepped out of their careers have an intense fear of putting themselves "back out there," especially when they lack experience with the latest technology used in their field. They aren't sure they can catch up and learn the skills necessary to function in today's workplace. This lack of self-confidence compounds the fear that the world has moved on without them. Their limiting belief is that there is no way to catch up.

"I am paralyzed, stuck." Midlife often brings changes to the foundational relationships, activities, and roles that once defined our lives. In the midst of change and upheaval, some women end up feeling stuck in a midlife paralysis. A common fear and limiting belief is that all our opportunities are gone and no one wants our experience, time, or giftings. The sentiment expressed by many women is, "I feel paralyzed. How can I contribute—to society, the church, or other people—when no one seems interested in what I have to offer?"

"I will be alone." As children leave the nest, loneliness and the fear of being alone become realities for many women at halftime. Some feel panicked when they look to the future and imagine

year after year of an empty house with no children. These fears are compounded for women who have experienced or are currently navigating the loss of a spouse through divorce or death, or who are facing the end of other significant relationships. Their fear is a lifetime of loneliness, and their limiting belief is that they are unable to build new and meaningful relationships.

While all the women we've coached have struggled with fears and limiting beliefs such as these, they have also found ways to move beyond them. And identifying fears and limiting beliefs is the first essential step for moving beyond them.

THE SOURCES AND CONSEQUENCES OF OUR LIMITATIONS

Fear blocks our way from moving forward. Some of these fears and limiting beliefs are very real, and some are perceived, as if etched into our midlife DNA by life experience and past failures and wounds. In order to let go of these hindrances, we need to understand both their origins and their consequences.

The Sources of Fears and Limiting Beliefs

SHAYNE

Although both men and women have fears and limiting beliefs, women have unique experiences that can form such beliefs. Some of these are related to traumatic events, such as rape, domestic violence, verbal abuse, gaslighting, and misogyny. Others may not meet the definition of *traumatic* but are still a powerful source of negative beliefs. These might include difficulties experienced in childhood, being alienated from a group of friends or from family, being teased or mocked, or being "canceled" on social media. Although some might consider these to be more subtle sources of fear, the limiting beliefs they create are far from subtle. In fact, they can be spirit breaking and often incredibly confusing.

Our fears and limiting beliefs are a misguided form of self-protection, our psyche's way of keeping us safe from risk and harm. When it comes to pursuing a dream or even identifying one, we might encounter limiting beliefs because we fear we will pay a price if we speak our truth and live into the fullness of who God made us to be. We might fear we will be ostracized, lose favor, damage relationships, or miss opportunities. However, to keep moving forward, we need to take a closer look at these kinds of harmful self-talk to assess whether they're even true. To do that, it's often helpful to trace our fears and limiting beliefs back to their source. Once we understand where they come from, we can flip the script for a better outcome in our second half.

I faced this issue in my halftime process when I got stuck and couldn't move forward. Carolyn helped me realize I was wrestling with a fear of failure and of feeling like a fraud. When she asked me where that belief came from, I recalled a difficult experience from twenty years earlier.

I was in my early thirties when I was invited to attend a two-day seminar led by a high-profile pastor and leader. I was working on a master's in theology at the time and was beyond excited about the opportunity to learn from someone who was so accomplished in ministry. In fact, I was geeking out at the privilege of being included in this exclusive gathering, which was limited to 300 people.

The seminar included times of teaching, question-and-answer sessions, and intense small group discussions. I was captivated by the theological exchanges and everything I was learning. However, I was also the only woman invited to attend, and I felt it. While no one was overtly unkind to me, I was treated differently. I was not a threat to the young men attending, but neither was I of any significance to them. I felt tolerated but not included. I got the sense that they believed I would most likely not go on to lead a church, teach the Scriptures, or have responsibilities for shepherding others as they would. I strongly suspected they viewed me as being there for my own self-actualization, as if my theological studies were a hobby rather than a means for me to serve the church and the world.

As I absorbed all these messages and processed them into limiting beliefs, I began to feel self-conscious and insecure. Despite my experience and education, I felt like a fraud. As the seminar went on, these feelings only intensified—and I felt there was evidence to back them up. When I spoke up in discussions with other participants, I was listened to politely, but my ideas were consistently skipped over as the group moved on to the next idea—the next man's idea. At the end of each session, groups of participants clustered up and continued talking, but I had no one to talk to or process with. I felt invisible and alone.

During a break between sessions, I holed up in a stall in the women's restroom and broke down. I spent the next fifteen minutes crying with my head pressed against the side of the metal stall. No one was threatening me, but I was filled with fear. *I don't belong here. They think I'm a joke. Why am I even trying?*

Unfortunately, it felt like my fears and limiting beliefs were fully realized in the next session. I decided to take one last risk and raised my hand to respond to a question posed by the pastor leading the seminar. Instead of taking me seriously, he laughed at my answer—and then so did the 300 men in attendance. My contribution was publicly mocked. At the next break, I left the seminar a day early and didn't go back.

As Carolyn and I talked through this memory and the

significance of it, I realized that what had originally sent me to the bathroom stall crying was my own fears and limiting beliefs, which then became the lens through which I viewed everything else.

To be fair, I do not recall what the pastor's question was, nor do I remember my answer. It may well have been hilarious. And yet, this hurtful experience solidified into an insurmountable barricade that persisted for more than twenty years. Did this high-profile teacher also laugh at the comments of the men who sat in the room? Maybe. If so, was it seen as playful? Perhaps. Was he laughing at me in the same way? I don't know.

I now believe the answers to these questions don't really matter. What matters is that once I understood its source, I could move past the limiting belief that I was a fraud and did not have anything substantial to contribute to the church and the world. I could move forward without discouragement and keep trying to find my place.

The Consequences of Fears and Limiting Beliefs

Unaddressed fears and limiting beliefs have the power to derail your halftime journey and rob you of a second half full of joy and purpose. They can keep you from setting and achieving goals, and from looking for opportunities and relationships that might be a good fit for you. They can also contribute to depression, anxiety, and even panic attacks. The *Archives of Internal Medicine* published findings that after the age of fifty, women are more at risk for suffering from panic attacks, especially if there is undealt-with past trauma or fear. In their study they found that:

- 18 percent had experienced panic attacks in the past six months.

- 13 percent had panic attacks severe enough to impair their social activities and daily lives.

- 7 percent had limited-symptom panic attacks that manifested with rapid or irregular heartbeats only.

- 14 percent had full-blown panic attacks. The majority were experienced by women between ages fifty to fifty-nine.[2]

Limiting beliefs are no joke, and although your past experiences and the messages lodged in your subconscious can be a beast to wrangle, you have the power, with the aid of the Holy Spirit, to replace limiting beliefs with empowering beliefs that will serve you better and provide a bedrock for your second half. This process is not one that will happen overnight. It takes intentionality, self-awareness, and work to replace a possible lifetime of subconscious self-talk. But in the process, you will essentially be rewiring your brain and creating new neural pathways that bypass the limiting beliefs.

Take a moment to consider any limiting beliefs you hold about yourself. For example, you may feel, as Cristin did, that you can't catch up with a professional world that has moved on without you, especially if you took time out of your career to raise children. This belief might once have served you by keeping you content in the path you were on, but it no longer does now that your children have left home. The belief that you can't catch up is holding you back from new possibilities for your future—this is the consequence in your life. However, as we discuss in the next section, it is possible to replace limiting beliefs with empowering beliefs. In this case, the new truth from Scripture you might embrace is, "I can do all things through Christ who strengthens me" (Philippians 4:13, NKJV).

Again, know that you have power over your own thoughts and beliefs. God is light and truth, and through him you can learn to see beyond the distortions of fear and limiting beliefs. Don't let them hold you back and keep you from fully committing to new relationships, to yourself, to the Lord, and to your new future.

FACE YOUR FEARS AND LIMITING BELIEFS

Leaving behind the false assumptions that hold you back requires identifying them, processing them, and then replacing them with empowering beliefs. Over time, the goal is to rewire the way you think so you are free to pursue your dreams for a fulfilling second half.

"All of us are going to have a different lie playing in our head to keep us down. Mine is that I am not doing enough. Because for years, my life was all about getting things done every day, successfully accomplishing something in my business."

Lisa Payne, *former Fortune 500 CFO*

Identify your barriers. Depending on where you are in your halftime journey, you may already be well aware of your fears and limiting beliefs. However, if you aren't yet sure what they might be, begin by identifying a step you want to take or a decision you need to make to move your life forward. What hindering thoughts come to mind when you think about taking that step or making that decision? Another option is to become a student of your self-talk as you go about your day. What negative statements play on repeat in your thinking? These are all clues to the fears that fuel your limiting beliefs.

Process your defeatist thoughts. Once you have identified your obstacles, it is essential to expose them and bring them into the light. We recommend talking them through with a trusted friend, counselor, or coach. Share the fears and limiting beliefs you identified. Invite the other person to help you analyze them and identify their source. Just saying them aloud often diminishes their power. Continue processing by sharing them with God in prayer, asking him to renew your mind and to focus your thoughts on "what is true, and honorable, and right" (Philippians 4:8).

Replace your fears and limiting beliefs with empowering beliefs. Once you have identified and processed your fears and limiting beliefs, the next step is to replace them with empowering beliefs. This is how you flip the script for better outcomes in your life. Here's an example of what it looks like to do that.

Limiting Beliefs	Empowering Beliefs
My best years are behind me.	My future will be the best years of my life.
My body will never be the same.	My aging body is beautiful and a gift from God.
I am professionally incompetent.	I will learn and flourish in the world.
I am paralyzed, stuck.	There are wide-open spaces out there for me to find where I will move forward in freedom.
I will be alone.	I will find, nurture, and sustain meaningful relationships.

Use the chart on page 110—or recreate it in your journal—to replace your limiting beliefs with empowering beliefs. If you find it helpful, you may wish to make identifying empowering beliefs part of your processing conversation with a friend, counselor, or coach.

Although this exercise may seem simple, replacing limiting beliefs with empowering beliefs is an ongoing process. Chances

Limiting Beliefs	Empowering Beliefs

are, you will take one step forward and then a couple of steps back as you create new beliefs and self-talk to throw off what entangles you. Give yourself grace to keep trying, and trust that progress will come. Like so many women we've coached, you really can move beyond fear and limiting beliefs. With God's help, you can develop an empowering mindset to help you keep moving to the next level of significance for your life.

FIND FREEDOM

Cristin did the hard work that enabled her to break free from the limiting belief that her learning days were over and that technology had forever passed her by. She rewired her thinking and embraced the truth that she could learn at any age, and that she could even have fun in the process.

When she realized that self-doubt and perfectionism were holding her back, she identified and broke free from another fear, which was her fear of failure. "The fear of failure is a real thing, but it is part of the process," Cristin explains. "I've learned there is actually no such thing as failure. It is all just information I can use to pivot from something that is not working to something that will work."

The more Cristin found freedom from fears and limiting beliefs that were holding her back, the more clarity she gained about her dream. Cristin founded a coaching and consulting company and created an online course to give struggling families resources that did not leave them in an endless cycle of counseling. She applied her education and the experience she'd gained building teams in corporate America to help families build their own strong teams, teaching them how to create a blueprint for success and connection.

But none of it would have happened if Cristin hadn't let go of her fears and limiting beliefs. "I had to get free from the feeling that I had missed my opportunity, that it was too late," she says. Today, Cristin embraces who she is at her core: unique and wired to see the world through the eyes of a strategic, futuristic soul.

ESSENTIAL PRACTICES

PRAY

Share. In God's presence, name the past experiences, beliefs, or messages that have contributed to your fears and limiting beliefs. If forgiveness and healing are needed, ask God for these things.

Ask. Invite God to help you see the truths and empowering beliefs on the other side of your fears and limiting beliefs. Ask him to help you believe that you really can replace limiting beliefs with empowering beliefs.

Listen. Ask God to help you let go of any beliefs that do not serve you in your second half. Listen for God's prompting and surrender your fears to him.

ACT

- Complete the exercises described in "Face Your Fears and Limiting Beliefs" (pages 108–110).

- Choose one fear or limiting belief and trace it back to its source. Journal your responses to the following questions.

  » What experience comes to mind when you think about this fear or limiting belief?

» How did the experience impact you at the time? How does it continue to impact you now?

» In what ways does this fear or limiting belief provide misguided self-protection? How does it keep you from moving forward?

ADJUST

Based on what you've learned from taking action, what adjustments do you want to make? Consider any adjustments in your thoughts and beliefs that could help you move forward. Write them in your journal.

CREATE CAPACITY FOR
YOUR NEW PATH FORWARD

*If you stay so busy, or you don't psychologically let go of
what you're doing and mourn it, then it's going to be very hard for
you to take on something else. Otherwise, it's just crowded in there.
And I think we filter things. We don't even see opportunities in front
of us when we're so up to our ears in what we're doing.*

MARGIE BLANCHARD, PRESIDENT AND COFOUNDER,
KEN BLANCHARD COMPANIES

For more than twenty-five years, Dr. J. J. Smith had personally
counseled patients and managed a dedicated group of caregivers at
a university hospital. Like many healthcare professionals, she'd had
to navigate complex changes in this industry that seemed to happen almost daily. And the pressure to spend less time with patients
to drive profits and productivity higher was both relentless and
demoralizing. As J. J. resisted the demands she felt compromised
her ability to do her job well, she got the impression she was no
longer appreciated by management. She had cared deeply for her
patients and her staff, but things were changing, and she realized
it was time for her to move on.

J. J. was in her early sixties and decided to retire, but she also wanted to keep the door open for the next thing God might have for her. As it happened, she was in the process of renovating her home during this time and decided to do something about two enormous oak trees that overwhelmed her yard. The original owners had planted the trees too close to the house. Now that they had grown for decades, they threatened the house's structure. Additionally, J. J. was worried one might come crashing down on the house in a storm. The trees also took up space that she could use for something more beautiful and useful, like a sunroom.

J. J. hired a contractor to remove the trees and watched him use his chain saw to cut them down. Then she had an idea. Rather than simply being a bystander, she asked if she could join him in cutting up the trunk and branches. She wanted to be part of the process of creating space for something new.

It's important to note that J. J. is petite and weighs about 110 pounds. So she asked for a small chain saw, something she could safely wield. After overcoming his surprise at her request, the contractor found one. Together, they dispatched with the giant oak trees, which for J. J. had become a symbol of a past that no longer worked for her. She now refers to the work she did that day as her "chain-saw therapy."

The physical work of getting rid of something that was taking up space in her life inspired her to look for the "oak tree" equivalents in other areas of her life. She began by evaluating everything on her schedule that was simply taking up space. After doing the hard work of removing what no longer served her, J. J. was able to live a more intentional and joy-filled life. Chain-saw therapy gave her the creative motivation to see opportunities that had previously been crowded out by the things that no longer belonged in her second half.

FOUR COMPONENTS OF CAPACITY

While we don't recommend chain-saw therapy for everyone, we do recommend being intentional about creating capacity for something new. Capacity is your ability to do something or the amount of something you can hold in your life. Because your time and resources are limited, creating capacity requires eliminating some things to make room for others. That's how you open space in your life to explore new opportunities, especially when your previous way of life is changing.

Here's a description of capacity that's both humorous and memorable: "If your bird cage is at full *capacity*, you can't stuff one more feathered friend in there without causing birdie claustrophobia."[1] Birdie claustrophobia is a fitting image because when we talk about capacity, we mean having the space you need to live out your dream in practical ways. If you do not create capacity, the claustrophobia of an overcommitted life will smother your dreams. Halftime Institute founder Bob Buford puts it this way:

> "*I was a doer. I was busy as a mom, wife, employee, daughter, and friend. I didn't have time for me. I longed for more purpose and meaning in my life. My biggest obstacle was distraction. I had too much going on and I couldn't see the forest for the trees.*"
>
> Debra Dean, PhD, *organizational leadership*

Desire alone will not allow you to do something new in your second half. You must create the capacity to do it. If you're being controlled by too many time- and energy-consuming activities, you will continue to be frustrated by unfulfilled dreams and desires.[2]

To create capacity, we encourage the women we coach to take a metaphorical chain saw to four areas of their lives—their time, their mental space, their finances, and their spiritual life.

Time Capacity

Creating capacity with time is often one of the most significant challenges women face. It typically requires letting go of roles and responsibilities that no longer fit or feel life-giving. Busyness affects every aspect of our lives—work, relationships, health, our ability to connect with God, everything. When women are in a season of transition, the temptation is to take on more tasks to fill the gaps. We can always be busier, but that is not the goal.

The goal is to be wise by pausing to evaluate what is currently on your calendar and assess what needs to be subtracted before adding something else. This is as essential for the stay-at-home mom as it is for the woman working full time outside the home. Creating margin in your schedule gives you the time you need to see and act beyond your day-to-day obligations, which is essential for discovering and pursuing your calling. Then you will be able to make intentional changes because you'll have the time to explore what fits and what does not.

Creating time capacity can be especially tricky for empty-nesting, stay-at-home moms who come to midlife and feel they have way too much capacity already. For many moms, this can lead to boredom and discouragement. Again, the challenge is to resist the temptation to simply fill up the time with different activities in order to be intentional about choosing activities that are the right fit.

Similarly, women who come to midlife having worked full time for years often experience busyness as a drug—they depend on it to feel productive and significant. If this describes you, know that you may be especially vulnerable to the temptation to jump from one form of busyness to another without creating space to fully explore your next steps.

Whether you have been in the corporate world, a stay-at-home mom, or a hybrid of the two, we encourage you to get a baseline by tracking how you spend your time over the course of an average week. Think of it as a time budget, one in which everyone on the planet has exactly the same amount to spend as you do. Just as you review how you spend your money to stay on budget financially, keep track of how and where you spend your waking hours each day. After one week, highlight the activities that are most important to you. These are your nonnegotiables. Now look at the rest of your time budget and consider what you can eliminate to create more capacity in your calendar.

Mental Capacity

Creating mental capacity is what gives you emotional and psychological space to dream. One of the ways you create mental capacity is by letting go of your first-half identity and having the courage to see yourself with new eyes in your second half. Creating mental capacity requires stepping out of life on autopilot so you can pause, analyze your capacity, and assess why you are doing what you are doing. For example, while you will always be a mom, mothering adult children who have left the nest will look vastly different from your carpool and PTA days. Or if you have been a Fortune 500 C-suite executive who is used to having every waking moment of your day scheduled, you may have to significantly pare down your calendar in order to have the mental space you need to consider what's next for you.

Getting free and creating mental capacity means opening your mind to divinely inspired possibilities for your future. This requires making time for prayer and doing an honest assessment of your potential and opportunities. You protect your time, your gifts, and your ability to discern your next steps when you have the mental space you need to pray and think things through. If you give yourself too quickly to people and places that are not aligned with your life-giving Ephesians 2:10 calling, you'll only delay finding your best fit. Every yes you say to one thing is a no you say to something else. Take the time you need to thoroughly consider your responsibilities and opportunities with fresh eyes.

Financial Capacity

Having financial capacity means living in such a way that you are managing your money instead of your money managing you. Ideally, it means having financial margin that frees you up to give yourself to a cause or purpose that's bigger than you.

One of the misconceptions some have is that you have to be wealthy to successfully launch your second half—that you must be a rich person with lots of time to spare. However, living out your Ephesians 2:10 calling is more about availability than affluence. Many women continue to work full-time or part-time jobs as part of living their dream. Others, like Dr. J. J. Smith, can retire or have other means of supporting themselves while they do volunteer work.

Whether or not you work, finances are a factor in being able to do what you feel called to do. Halftime Institute founder Bob Buford used to say it's hard to get clear on your calling when you're cash-flow negative.

If finances are tight or you're burdened with debt, the prospect of freeing up capacity with your money may create insecurity and fear. If so, we invite you to start by leaning into an abundance mindset rather than a scarcity mindset. God's purpose for your life can't be thwarted by a lack of funds. You join with him in pursuing financial freedom by simply taking your next best step to manage your money so your money isn't managing you. That might be anything from reading a book about debt reduction to taking an online course in budgeting to consulting a financial professional for guidance. In fact, before acting on any financial plan, we encourage you to meet with a trustworthy financial planner (someone who won't try to sell you anything) to help you make wise decisions with your money.

Once you're managing your money, the capacity questions to ask are:

- How much is enough? How much money do you need to meet your essential expenses?

- What spending can you eliminate or reduce to create more capacity? Focus on the small cuts as well as larger ones. Every dollar counts.

- What lifestyle changes might you make to create more financial capacity?

For most of us, creating financial capacity will require creating or adjusting a budget and sticking to it over time. Don't let that discourage you. Instead, remember that if the God of all resources has empowered your calling, he will also provide the resources. Again, this requires having a mindset of abundance rather than scarcity, and also careful planning. Remember, foundational components of the halftime journey are embracing change and seeking wise counsel to help you along the way. Every time you are willing to adjust—to be flexible and open—you take a step closer to joy, hope, and energy. God wants to partner with you in your finances. You demonstrate your trust in his provision when you take even one step forward.

Spiritual Capacity

While freeing up spiritual capacity might initially seem similar to freeing up mental capacity, they are actually very distinct from each other. Creating mental capacity gives you emotional and psychological space to consider new paths forward. Spiritual capacity is about tapping into the power of the Almighty and the flow of the Holy Spirit to empower you.

You create spiritual capacity to live out your purpose by keeping your spiritual tank filled to overflowing. That means creating space and time for practices such as prayer, meditation, reading, learning, or other methods of growth that help you to feel spiritually alive. As a starting point, many women we coach have taken a solo, silent retreat to pause and decompress. A retreat might be a few hours or a few days in a peaceful environment that calms your emotions and spirit. Anything you can do to create spiritual capacity is important because, again, you cannot live out your Ephesians 2:10 calling—God's dream for your life—without him.

One of the greatest challenges in creating spiritual capacity is a disease that can debilitate your spiritual health. Author John Ortberg refers to it as "hurry sickness" and recalls the remedy once prescribed by a wise friend who said, "You must ruthlessly eliminate hurry from your life." Ortberg goes on to say, "Hurry is the great enemy of spiritual life in our day. Hurry can destroy our souls. Hurry can keep us from living well. As Carl Jung wrote, 'Hurry is not *of* the devil; hurry *is* the devil.'"[3]

Although we may never completely eradicate hurry from our lives, we can learn from the master, Jesus, who never seemed to be in a rush. Even when the weight of the world was on his shoulders, Jesus took time away from the crowds to meet with the Father (Mark 1:35; 6:31). Instead of allowing a depleted spiritual tank, he kept his tank filled to overflowing by carving out time to be alone with God.

One way to know that you have created spiritual capacity is when you are able to feel peace of heart and mind, regardless of your circumstances. Peace that doesn't make any logical sense is peace from a divine power source. This is why Paul said, "Do not be anxious about anything, but in everything by prayer and pleading with thanksgiving let your requests be made known to God. And the peace of God, which surpasses all comprehension, will guard your hearts and minds in Christ Jesus" (Philippians 4:6-7, NASB).

To live out your Ephesians 2:10 calling, you need spiritual capacity to tap into God's power source for your best life.

CREATE CAPACITY FOR SOMETHING NEW

Creating capacity for something new at midlife truly is a partnership with God. While he supplies the power, you must make the choices to open up your time, mental space, financial resources, and spiritual capacity. And making those decisions can be hard because most of us resist change and gravitate toward the familiar. Even when we want change at some level, we also want comfortable, safe places and desire to be with people and in environments where we feel we belong.

To overcome the natural resistance we all feel toward change, it's important to flip your internal narrative. There are three practices you can use to help you do that: normalize endings and new beginnings, step boldly toward the unfamiliar, and open your mind to new possibilities. Rather than resisting change, think of it as moving toward adventure. You are creating space, opening new capacity for your next season by embracing this unfamiliar terrain.

Normalize Endings and New Beginnings

In his book *Necessary Endings*, Dr. Henry Cloud states:

> Endings are not only part of life; they are a requirement
> for living and thriving, professionally and personally.
> Being alive requires that we sometimes kill off things
> in which we were once invested, uproot what we
> previously nurtured, and tear down what we built
> for an earlier time.[4]

Dr. Margie Blanchard understands what it takes to uproot what she had previously nurtured and to move on to the next assignment in life. She entered her midlife transition fully invested in a life of service with deep roots in the leadership development business she ran with her husband, Ken. She loved her work as president of the Ken Blanchard Companies because it felt more like a ministry than a job.

Margie hit her halftime transition when a vague feeling of discontent eventually became full-blown weariness. She had been president of the company for eleven years, and she was burning out. When she finally admitted that she needed to stop doing this job and do something else, she felt at a loss about what she wanted to do. That's when Margie began working with a coach who provided accountability and a program to help her keep moving. She knew accountability was critical because while doing the work of change was necessary, it was not always urgent. If she didn't have someone creating urgency to change, she knew she could drift for a long time in the familiar.

Part of Margie's accountability involved answering the question, "What are the biggest obstacles holding you back from moving forward?" The first answer was time capacity. Margie knew that people in transition usually focus first on what they can add to their schedules. Instead, she needed to create a vacuum in her schedule and mental space to explore the possibility of a new path. So Margie wrote a letter to herself and symbolically resigned.

The resignation letter created mental space for her even though she didn't immediately make other changes. In fact, she kept her office and assistant because she was not sure what was next. She put the letter in a drawer, did not tell anyone about it, and gave herself time to mourn. Even though she had loved her job, she had to admit she was tired of it. It was depleting her of energy. She also knew that making changes in her life would change other people's lives—including stakeholders and loved ones. This feeling of responsibility toward the people who mattered most weighed on her heart, and she needed time to grieve those losses as well.

Creating mental space allowed Margie to process all her future options and grieve her first half. This was important because she had to mentally let go of her past role and responsibilities, and even her past identity, to allow new things into her life. Getting free required facing her greatest obstacles head-on and getting clear on what was holding her back, which included fears both real and perceived. But somewhere deep inside her, Margie knew these changes could be meaningful and an adventure, and she was willing to embrace an ending to free herself for a new beginning.

Endings are a *requirement* for new beginnings. Before we can fully enter into the joy of our next season, we must leave some things behind and actively uproot others. To do so, Dr. Cloud suggests taking an inventory of what is working and what isn't—whatever is depleting you and your resources—and then ending whatever is necessary in order to move on. You normalize endings and new beginnings when you mentally free yourself from doing what you have always done.

Step Boldly toward the Unfamiliar

Transformational change requires taking action, which often means stepping boldly toward the unfamiliar. We have a compelling example of this from the life of the apostle Paul. After ministering together with friends for three years, Paul felt called to leave a place and people he loved and knew well.

> From Miletus, Paul sent to Ephesus for the elders of the church. When they arrived, he said to them: "You know how I lived the whole time I was with you, from the first day I came into the province of Asia. I served the Lord with great humility and with tears and in the midst of severe testing by the plots of my Jewish opponents. You know that I have not hesitated to preach anything that would be helpful to you but have taught you publicly and from house to house. I have declared to both Jews and Greeks that they must turn to God in repentance and have faith in our Lord Jesus.

> And now, *compelled by the Spirit, I am going to*
> *Jerusalem, not knowing what will happen to me there.*
> ACTS 20:17-22, NIV, EMPHASIS ADDED

Paul understood what it meant to step boldly toward the unfamiliar. He did not allow his love for what was familiar to keep him from pursuing his calling.

If you find yourself clinging to what is familiar because everything else in life feels out of control, you are not alone. Women in midlife often feel change averse because their everyday life is already changing or under threat of change. But it is possible to make another choice. Compelled by the Spirit, you can choose the adventure of stepping boldly toward the unfamiliar, trusting that your calling will be waiting for you there.

Open Your Mind to New Possibilities

A month after Margie did a brave heart check and wrote her symbolic resignation letter, things began to change. As if by divine intervention, innovative ideas for leadership and fresh opportunities came her way. Intentionally creating space in her mind, heart, and schedule led Margie and two colleagues to create an "Office of the Future" for the firm. It would be a think tank focused on keeping the company agile and prepared for upcoming technological changes in their industry.

After discussing this with her husband, Margie then officially stepped out of her role as company president and stepped into her future to lead this initiative. Although it was not a giant leap into something completely different, Margie's shift freed her to thrive and to grow in a new way that brought excitement to her life.

Opening your mind to possibilities can happen in any number

of ways. As it was for Margie, it might mean imagining your life without your current job or routine. It might mean taking a break from a toxic relationship or environment. It could also mean being willing to say yes to opportunities or experiences to which you might previously have said an automatic no.

Allow yourself to be creative. Envision a scenario that might replace your current reality. Walk through a day with your mind attuned to possibilities, some of which may be right in front of you. Give yourself permission to imagine your future in a new way.

IDENTIFY THREE PATHS FORWARD

As part of being open to new possibilities, we want to challenge you to identify three potential paths forward from where you are now. Even if you don't yet know what your dream is, this exercise is where your dream may start to take shape. And we want to help you give shape to it in a practical way, which is to focus on how much capacity you might need to pursue each of those paths.

If identifying three paths forward feels a little overwhelming at this point, allow us to put your mind at ease. You're not committing to anything; you're just allowing yourself to imagine three options for moving forward. For now, this activity is less about the paths themselves and more about beginning to think about the capacity required to move forward.

As you creatively consider three paths forward for your next season, one might be the path you are already on. Another might be a one- or two-degree shift in a project or role within your current company, ministry, or platform. Yet another way forward might be a "reach," a path that seems too big for you but not too big for God. The challenge is to take your dreams and factor in the time, mental, financial, and spiritual capacity you need for each path. The following three charts provide an example of what this looked like for one woman in our coaching program.

Path 1: Continue my current path as a real estate broker	
Time Capacity	This path requires 60 to 80 hours of work per week.
Mental Capacity	Honestly, this path allows almost no time to open my mind to new possibilities. But I could set boundaries to take off one weekend a month to rest and consider new possibilities.
Financial Capacity	Staying the course creates significant financial capacity for my family, leading to greater financial security. My next step could be to meet with a financial planner to set a goal for scaling back our spending so we can save more. We need to ask, "How much is enough?"
Spiritual Capacity	This path leaves me spiritually depleted. I don't often have a quiet time with my Creator, and my spiritual capacity feels like it's at zero. I could create capacity during my one weekend a month to have a silent retreat. Time alone with God would recharge my spiritual batteries.

Path 2: Become a full-time speaker and author, working in at-risk communities	
Time Capacity	I would need to give up my real estate business to pursue my dream of full-time writing and speaking at ministry retreats and conferences.
Mental Capacity	Before quitting my job, I would need at least one day a week to begin developing ideas for conference talks and articles I want to write.
Financial Capacity	Because speaking engagements may be inconsistent until I am more established, I will need to have eight to ten months of income saved to tide us over in the short term, and a clear plan to sustain us for the long term.
Spiritual Capacity	In order to create talks and write articles and books, I will need significant time for prayer and spiritual growth. I'd like to have an hour a day for prayer and journaling, a monthly retreat day, and an annual retreat week.

Path 3: Reduce hours in my real estate work to make time for ministry work	
Time Capacity	I could cut my real estate hours to 32 hours a week to retain full-time benefits while still freeing up 8 hours a week for ministry speaking and writing.
Mental Capacity	During those 8 hours, I can commit to 2 hours per week for the mental space I need to create encouraging content for my ministry community, while also allowing me to put self-care on the priority list.
Financial Capacity	A 32-hour work week will require sacrifices but will not put my family at financial risk. We would need an agreed-upon budget. We will also need to meet with a financial planner who can help us look at long-term sustainability.
Spiritual Capacity	This path would give me more time to meet with the Lord and press into my own spiritual development. I would need to have a daily quiet time with the Lord, 45 minutes per day, to fill my spiritual tank.

Now it's your turn. As you imagine your three paths forward, it is important to make this exercise your own. Only you know what your capacity requirements might be. By doing this work up front, you will be one step closer to making your dreams a reality.

Path 1:	
Time Capacity	
Mental Capacity	

Financial Capacity	
Spiritual Capacity	

Path 2:	
Time Capacity	
Mental Capacity	
Financial Capacity	
Spiritual Capacity	

Path 3:	
Time Capacity	
Mental Capacity	
Financial Capacity	
Spiritual Capacity	

Creating capacity is about having enough time, money, and mental and spiritual energy to joyfully love and serve others while also loving yourself by moving forward. Having margin in your life opens up the possibility of exploring new paths with the resources you need to follow God's direction.

NEW CAPACITY, NEW LIFE

Following her chain-saw therapy with the enormous oak trees that crowded her property, J. J. Smith sat for a moment to take in her wide-open space, a visual representation of the new capacity she wanted in her second half. In that moment, J. J. remembered someone who had not been on her priority list for years—herself. In caring for patients, family, and friends in need, she had neglected the things that she loved to do just for fun. She loved anything in nature: hiking, kayaking, biking, spending time with the Lord outside, especially near bodies of water. Over the years, she and her husband had tried to fit in these activities when there was time, which was rarely.

In her new season, J. J. decided to put self-care at the top of her priority list, right under time with the Lord, giving herself unhurried hours and days to reclaim her love for life. And if you're wondering what she ultimately decided to put in the place freed up by removing those oak trees, the answer is: nothing. J. J. chose to keep the space open, which would remind her to cherish and protect the mental space she needed to be open for new possibilities.

It takes time to create new capacity, so give yourself the time you need—and put yourself back at the top of your priority list. It takes prayer to discern whether something is worth investing your time and energy in. Creating margin in your calendar will empower you to discover and pursue your calling. Having time to think and act outside of your current day-to-day obligations will help you make the changes you want. It may take internal or actual resignations from what no longer is your perfect fit. And you may need your own version of chain-saw therapy in the process. But when you take a bold step to cut down what no longer has a place in your life, you will be free to embrace God's unique plan, the plan designed in advance just for you.

ESSENTIAL PRACTICES

PRAY

Share. Be honest with God about any struggles or emotions you have in connection with creating capacity. Share any concerns about making changes in the areas of your time, money, mental space, and spiritual health. He cares about all of them.

Ask. God is the God of all resources, and he has more than enough to make your dreams a reality. What do you need most from him right now? Ask him to provide for you.

Listen. What do you sense God may be whispering to you? Listen for his wisdom, his insights, and his care and concern for you.

ACT

- Complete the exercise described in "Identify Three Paths Forward" (pages 128–132). Then journal your responses to the following questions.

  » As you consider your three paths forward, which one generates the greatest feeling of joy for you?

  » What other feelings were you aware of as you completed the charts?

  » What, if anything, surprised you about the capacity you might need to move forward?

- For a seven-day period, keep a time diary, tracking how you spend each hour of the day. At the end of the seven days, review your entries. Highlight the activities that are most important to you. Then create a time budget, prioritizing what you want to keep and eliminating what you can to create more capacity.

- Journal your responses to the following questions about the four components of capacity.

  » *Time capacity*. What's the biggest obstacle you face when it comes to creating time capacity?

  » *Mental capacity*. What would you do if you already had more mental capacity—more time to dream and be open to new possibilities?

  » *Financial capacity*. What would living at peace financially look like for you?

  » *Spiritual capacity*. What fills you up spiritually? What depletes you spiritually?

ADJUST

Based on what you've learned from taking action, what adjustments do you want to make? Consider any adjustments that would help you to create more time capacity, mental capacity, financial capacity, or spiritual capacity. Write them in your journal.

7

EMBRACE FORGIVENESS

I just found out my husband has been having an affair for six months. I knew he struggled with pornography, but I never thought he would betray me like this. I gave up everything to empower his career and to raise our family. I always knew the kids would grow up and leave, but I never planned to be all alone, without my husband, at this age.

ANONYMOUS

While Tana Greene was in her midlife transition, she attended a large church she loved. When the church launched a significant capital campaign at a weekend service, each member was asked to identify what they were good at and how they could contribute. Tana, a successful, well-known entrepreneur in her community, immediately stepped up.

After the service, Tana enthusiastically approached the senior pastor and said, "I'm good at leading. I want to help."

The pastor paused for a moment, seemingly taken aback by her offer. He then said, "Why don't we get you leading the cleaning crew."

Tana felt the sting. As the cofounder of two national staffing companies with a combined $80 million in annual revenue, Tana had something else in mind for how her gifts might help with the capital campaign.

To put this in perspective, Tana is a successful, thoughtful, and intelligent businesswoman with extensive experience in executive leadership. Recognized for her innovative business practices, she had once been invited to the White House to attend a forum for small business leaders, along with the president, Small Business Administration officials, legislators, and other leaders representing the twenty-nine million small businesses in the United States. Tana had a seat at the leadership table in the East Room of the White House but could not get a seat at the leadership table of her church.

While Tana was momentarily stopped in her tracks by her pastor's comment, she had learned a powerful lesson early on that was key to her phenomenal success. Forgive quickly and authentically, let go of offenses, then move on. Tana was able to walk away, not with bitterness or anger, but with grace, empowered by forgiveness.

This hadn't always been her story. Forgiveness was a hard lesson from her past, tied to trauma and mistreatment she'd experienced as a young wife and mother.

FORGIVENESS IS FOR YOU AND YOUR FUTURE

Forgiveness is a common concept in our language and culture, lifted up as a virtue when raising children, in our schools, and in our conflicts with friends and family, organizations or workplaces. It is understood that the practice of forgiveness is overall a good idea for society. As Christians, our understanding of forgiveness is foundational to our faith and has practical implications for how we live our lives and for our relationships. It is such a common concept that we may assume that everyone knows what forgiveness is, what is required to forgive, and why it is essential not only to the Christian life, but for our purposes here and for your halftime journey.

In his book *Mere Christianity*, author C. S. Lewis wrote, "Everyone says forgiveness is a lovely idea, until they have something to forgive."[1] This quote is even more poignant when one considers he wrote it in Europe in 1952, within the first decade after the end of World War II. He was writing to Christians of that time, urging them to forgive real horror and real evil done to their Jewish neighbors and anyone brave enough to help them. It goes without saying that this was not a popular idea among his peers at the time, to forgive the Nazis, yet he clung to his Christian faith and to the Christian doctrine of forgiveness, while advocating that accountability for the evil done is imperative and that justice must be sought.

It's rare for a woman to reach midlife without having someone she needs to forgive. For some women, it may be the person who wounded them through trauma, divorce, abuse, crime, addiction, racism, or any other form of harm. For others, it may be a difficult person in their life—a disengaged spouse, an overbearing parent, an angry in-law, a sibling who let them down, a friend who ghosted them, a coworker who took credit for their work. Or it may be that the person they most need to forgive is themselves. We have all hurt others and been hurt by them, which is why forgiveness is so important.

And yet, forgiveness is also complicated. Sometimes it's hard to acknowledge that there has been real pain in our life, that people we love have wronged us. Other times it feels as if forgiveness is letting the other person off the hook or diminishing the harm of what they did. Even when we want to forgive, as Tana did, we still sometimes struggle. While forgiveness is a decision, it rarely comes as easily as the flip of a switch. The deeper the harm or offense, the more time and hard work is required to truly and fully forgive. And so we often put it off, deny that we're holding resentments, or maybe even decide that what happened to us is simply unforgiveable. Sadly, when we choose unforgiveness, we are the ones who pay the biggest price. Author and psychologist Lewis Smedes wrote, "Without forgiving, we choke off our own joy; we kill our own soul."[2] We need to forgive because forgiveness is for us and our future. It is central to the Christian faith, and it is the only way to move forward.

Why You Need to Forgive

If you were raised attending Sunday school, you are likely familiar with verses such as "Be kind and compassionate to one another, forgiving each other, just as in Christ God forgave you" (Ephesians 4:32, NIV). This verse and others like it provide the biblical foundation for the Christian doctrine of forgiveness—that we are to forgive others because we ourselves have been forgiven. Just as God "does not treat us as our sins deserve or repay us according to our iniquities" (Psalm 103:10, NIV), we are to extend the mercy of forgiveness to others. We need to forgive because, to put it plainly, forgiveness is not optional for those who follow Christ.

> *"Living with someone who has cancer tests everything. It requires a new level of tenderness. I want to be quick to forgive because people will often say and do the wrong things when they don't know what to do."*
>
> Virginia Sambuco, *former customer care executive*

This is especially important for women at halftime because the goal is to pursue a life of joy and purpose, to live in a way that is most authentic to who God made you to be. This requires living according to your theology as much as it does living according to your true self and your values. What you believe is foundational for your halftime journey because you don't just *think* your theology, you *live* it.

This is why we invite the women we coach to begin processing forgiveness by first considering what they really believe about God. We want them to wrestle with questions like these:

- Do you believe that your faith—what you believe about God—is evident in how you live your life?

- Do you believe the gospel—that Jesus died on the cross to forgive you of your sins?

- Do you harbor resentments and unforgiveness toward anyone?

If the answer to that last question is yes, then we challenge women to consider another question: If you are holding on to past offenses and unforgiveness, how much do you really trust the gospel message?

Sounds a little harsh, right? And yet, it is also a compassionate question. We want the best for the women we coach. We want them to be free of whatever might keep them from moving toward their God-given dreams. But that won't happen if they are stuck in deep-seated resentments and unforgiveness.

When author C. S. Lewis was challenged by his peers about the notion of forgiving even the most heinous of crimes, he wrote this:

Right in the middle of [the Lord's Prayer], I find "Forgive us our sins as we forgive those that sin against us." There

is no slightest suggestion that we are offered forgiveness on any other terms. It is made perfectly clear that if we do not forgive we shall not be forgiven. There are no two ways about it. What are we to do?[3]

There is simply no way to gloss over unforgiveness. It's been said, "You deal with your stuff, or your stuff deals with you," which is another way of saying what you believe will manifest itself in your life. When unforgiveness goes unaddressed and unchecked, it can shut down joy and derail any progress toward purpose and freedom. It can end relationships, destroy families, poison work environments, and so much more. If you want to have a big, audacious, and fulfilling second half, forgiveness is the key that opens the floodgates to freedom. Just ask Tana Greene.

Tana was a sixteen-year-old wife and mother trying to make the best of a difficult marriage when it happened. She woke up one morning and made breakfast for herself and her family. She was getting ready for work when she walked out into the hallway and saw her husband standing there aiming a shotgun at her face.[4]

"Go ahead," he threatened. "Walk out that door."

Tana instantly fell to the floor in terror. She raised her hands above her head and begged for her life. She had seen the rage in his eyes and even heard him laugh. He kept her in this position, on the floor with a shotgun pointed at her head, for thirty minutes before finally letting her go. On another occasion, he hit her repeatedly across the face before finally dumping her and her baby boy in her parents' driveway, her face covered in blood.

She was traumatized, humiliated, and angry at what had been done to her but also determined to turn her life around. As a young woman, divorced just before her eighteenth birthday, she did her best to let go of resentment and bitterness toward her ex-husband and to move on with her life. More importantly, she worked to forgive herself for getting pregnant as a teen and staying in a dangerous situation. Forgiveness and the ability to move on became key to both her future and her very survival.

Tana was determined to do things differently. She set big goals: finish school, buy her own house by age twenty-five, marry a good man, and have her own business by thirty. Forgiveness opened Tana's heart to love. She married a kind man and even exceeded her goals. She truly believed she had moved on from this awful beginning of her adult life. But when she hit her midlife crisis, she realized she hadn't let go of the past as much as she thought she had.

Tana's midlife crisis followed the September 11, 2001, terrorist attacks in New York City. Like many companies, her manufacturing business felt the blow when financial repercussions rippled throughout the economy. Then her father passed away and she had health problems of her own. Tana hit a low point, and she knew she needed help. It seemed like one hit after another. To get help, she began working with a coach so she could not only process her past and present challenges, but also fully move on. Over the next two decades, Tana was able to pivot and rebuild her company into one of the fastest growing women-owned businesses in the United States. Tana took this part of her halftime journey seriously and did the work of forgiveness.

That's the beauty and grace of forgiveness for women at halftime—it releases you from your past and enables you to wholeheartedly live into your Ephesians 2:10 calling, which includes the good works God has prepared in advanced for you to do. For Tana, that calling began to take shape when a teacher friend who knew Tana's story asked her to speak to high school students in a healthy relationships class. Tana initially agreed but then had doubts. Although she had experienced horrific domestic violence, she felt unqualified to teach about it. She decided to go ahead and tell her story but to also bring along a domestic violence expert. That's how she met Karen Parker, president and CEO of Safe Alliance, the largest provider of care for victims of domestic violence in Charlotte, North Carolina, where Tana lived.[5]

After speaking to the students in the healthy relationships class, Karen and Tana went on to develop both a friendship and a partnership. Karen eventually asked Tana to join the Safe Alliance board. Tana felt deeply moved when she realized that her willingness to do the work of forgiveness was opening up a new calling on her life. In fact, in her role on the board, Tana ended up leading the agency's $10 million fund-raising campaign to build and open a new domestic violence shelter for women and families. Tana Greene, a woman who was passed over by her church, would go on to raise millions of dollars to help women escape and heal from domestic violence.

How Forgiveness Helps You Move Forward

When we are willing to do the work of forgiveness, it enables us to move forward to a fulfilling and joyful second half. That's how we free ourselves of the past. Psychotherapist Nancy Colier writes:

> Forgiveness, ultimately, is about freedom. When we need someone else to change in order for us to be OK, we are a prisoner. . . . What we want from the other, the one we can't forgive, is most often, love. Forgiveness is ultimately about choosing to offer ourselves love—and with it, freedom.[6]

When you make the decision to forgive, you cut the chains that shackle you to the past. This enables you to love freely, to establish boundaries, and to stay healthy as you move forward into your next season.

Forgiveness enables you to love freely. In your next season, harboring unforgiveness actually takes up the space that love wants to inhabit in your heart. Letting go of bitterness enables you to love again and to move on with your life. In his book *The Bait of Satan: Living Free from the Deadly Trap of Offense*, John Bevere argues that carrying resentments and unforgiveness from your past is how the enemy will take you down. These things are taking up mental and spiritual space and are preventing you from loving God and serving others fully. If you are someone who is easily offended and you write people off, or you make judgments because they say and do things you do not agree with, you are holding grudges against people in unforgiveness. If you are a person who is easily offended, you are leaking spiritually. As Beth Moore says, "Quit being so emotionally fragile. So hurt and offended all the time. Time to look ourselves in the mirror and say, 'Good grief, get over it.'"[7] Forgiveness feeds

"*I wrote three letters to each of my daughters: one sharing what I love most about them, another asking for forgiveness, and another expressing my hopes for our future together. I shared these letters throughout a special trip. I bought antique boxes so they could store the letters and included pictures of our family and their grandparents. It was kind of a living legacy for them.*"

Lisa Payne, former Fortune 500 CFO

your spiritual disciplines of grace and mercy toward others and toward yourself in order to love freely.

When you can authentically love others freely, without constant judgment or offense, it opens your life up to new relationships, connections, and opportunities. You will find a second half of joy and purpose begin to unfold effortlessly when you practice the discipline of forgiveness in your daily life against small and large offenses.

Forgiveness gives you boundaries. When we practice forgiveness, we learn to have boundaries and we can protect ourselves from the temptation of being easily offended. We begin to see that often others' words and actions have very little to do with us. The saying "hurt people hurt people" applies here. The grace and mercy toward others that begins to flourish in a mind practicing forgiveness creates boundaries when it comes to those who intentionally or unintentionally hurt you. You can have the healthy boundary to shake it off and to move on with your life in joy and purpose.

Some of us have experienced profound and life-changing trauma at the hands of others. It is important to note that forgiveness is never about minimizing or condoning what you have been through. To forgive is giving yourself permission to let it go and to get free from this person or group of people. Putting it down and leaving it forever takes the power away from the perpetrator, from the person or group, and from the enemy. Forgiveness is an invitation to break out of past trauma and break through to wide-open spaces in your heart, soul, and mind.

When you forgive, you establish healthy boundaries. Forgiveness frees you of bitterness, anger, and resentment; and healthy boundaries create a strong inner resolve to never again be in those situations when you have the power to not be. Boundaries say, "I will not ever submit to abuse. I will set positive intentions and goals for my life, not controlled by another. I will have wisdom to get out of bad relationships and situations, and I will learn to say no to toxic and abusive people in my life." Forgiveness and boundaries enable you to move on so that people and experiences from the past no longer have power over you.

Forgiveness keeps you healthy. Forgiveness helps to keep you in good health spiritually, emotionally, and physically. The benefits of forgiveness—of releasing resentments and the desire for revenge—are so profound that medical researchers have studied it. The Mayo Clinic lists multiple health benefits of forgiving:

- Healthier relationships

- Improved mental health

- Less anxiety, stress, and hostility

- Lower blood pressure

- Fewer symptoms of depression

- A stronger immune system

- Improved heart health

- Improved self-esteem[8]

These physical and emotional benefits, combined with a clear soul and a healthy spiritual life, will make you an unstoppable powerhouse in your second half. A spiritually healthy person loves others freely and accepts people, even with their imperfections. A spiritually healthy person has boundaries that protect her heart, soul, and mind. Forgiveness is empowering for your future.

Ultimately, we forgive because Christ has forgiven us. When we forgive others, we both honor our Savior and free ourselves to live a better life.

IDENTIFY WHO YOU NEED TO FORGIVE

The timing and process of forgiveness is unique to each person and each situation. As we offer some guidelines to help you begin this process, it's important to acknowledge that forgiving someone who caused a life-changing trauma will likely require more time, therapy, and prayer than forgiving someone who harmed you in a lesser way. The important thing is to forgive authentically. That's our objective in providing guidance—to help you to be ready for forgiveness, and to encourage you to keep moving forward in your process.

Schedule a block of time to be alone with God. Begin by setting aside time for prayer and reflection. Choose a quiet place where you won't be distracted. This could be in your church sanctuary during the week, a small chapel at a church, or a retreat center. If nature is a restful environment for you, choose a quiet spot at a park, in the woods, or by a lake where you can be alone with God. Any quiet place that feels safe and holy to you will work. Bring with you your Bible, a small pad of paper or sticky notes, an envelope, and something to write with. If you find it helpful to write out your prayers, you may also want to bring along your journal.

Once you arrive, settle into a comfortable position. Invite God to be with you and to guide you as you begin this process. You may wish to start by praying a psalm as an affirmation of God's protection and care for you, such as Psalm 23 or Psalm 121.

Acknowledge your pain. Pour out your heart to God and acknowledge the ways in which you feel wounded by the one(s) who harmed you. Share your grief and what each wound or offense has cost you. Take as much time as you need for this.

Write down the name(s). Use the small pad of paper or the sticky notes to write down the name or names of those you need to forgive—one name on each piece of paper.

Give them to God. Holding the paper names in your open palms, prayerfully surrender each one to God. You might pray, "Lord, I surrender [name] into your care. I want to forgive. Please help me."

To symbolize your surrender, you might fold the papers, seal them in the envelope, and then discard the envelope. You could crumple the names or make paper airplanes out of them and throw them in a trash can. If you are out in nature or your own backyard, you might dig a small hole, tear up the names, and bury them at the base of a tree. It doesn't matter how you symbolize your surrender. The important thing is to tangibly hand over to God the people you named.

Ask for what you need. Invite the Lord into any struggles you have. Ask for God's divine power to help you let go of unforgiveness. Pray for the strength you need to cut the chains that shackle you to those who have hurt you. Express your desire to be free from anger, resentment, and the desire for revenge.

Close your time by expressing your gratitude to God. Thank him for protecting you, for forgiving you, and for giving you the desire to forgive and to be free of the past.

If difficult emotions continue to surface in the days and weeks ahead, acknowledge them and surrender them again to God's care. When tempted to revisit your unforgiveness, pray for those you want to forgive, asking God to help you see them as he does. It is difficult to nurse resentment and anger toward someone while simultaneously bringing them before the Lord in prayer.

Practice forgiveness daily. Even if you need an extended period of time to forgive someone, don't let that keep you from practicing forgiveness in smaller ways with others. Think of it as forgiveness strength training, building up your forgiveness muscles by choosing to forgive the lesser offenses you might encounter each day. When someone cuts you off in traffic, forgive them and let go of the anger. When your spouse ignores you, process your emotions, then consider forgiveness as an alternative to an argument. If your friend won't take your call, consider your feelings, pray for them, and be the friend who doesn't hold a grudge. In addition, pray the Lord's Prayer regularly if you do not already do this as a part of your faith tradition. This is how Christ has taught us to pray:

Our Father, who art in heaven,
hallowed be thy Name,
thy kingdom come,
thy will be done,
on earth as it is in heaven.
Give us this day our daily bread.
And forgive us our trespasses,
as we forgive those
who trespass against us.
And lead us not into temptation,
but deliver us from evil.
For thine is the kingdom,
and the power, and the glory,
for ever and ever. Amen.[9]

AN ACCEPTABLE PAUSE IN THE PROCESS

CAROLYN

It's not uncommon for the women I coach to struggle with forgiveness. When it feels like they simply can't let go of the past, I advise clients to put their halftime work on hold in order to process their past and to do the work of forgiveness with a professional therapist. That is a perfectly acceptable pause in the process.

If you find yourself unable to open your mind, your heart, and your spirit to forgiveness, I encourage you to do the same—to take an acceptable pause and get professional counsel and care. As long as unforgiveness is taking up space in your heart, you won't have the space you need for joy and purpose.

Take the time you need to work through unforgiveness with a professional counselor or therapist. It may take six months, a year, or several years, but it is time well spent. This is your life. Trust that God will help you as you do the hard work to acknowledge your pain, to grieve, and to forgive.

Pausing your halftime work is not a failure or a sign of weakness. It is simply giving yourself the grace and time you need to be truly free.

THE LAND OF THE LIVING

In his work *Republic*, the ancient Greek philosopher Plato used the allegory of prisoners chained in a dark cave to reflect on the nature of human perception, knowledge, and education. However, it also functions as a compelling allegory of what happens when we are stuck in the dark cave of unforgiveness.

Plato's prisoners are chained in such a way that their backs are to the opening of the cave; they do not know an entrance is behind them, nor do they know what is on the other side of it. At the entrance to the cave burns a large fire that illuminates the activities of others who live freely outside the cave. The light of the fire casts flickering shadows against the back wall of the cave, the wall the prisoners are facing. The prisoners can see that life and activity is happening around them, but they see it only in shadows. This is the only reality they know, which C. S. Lewis famously called "the shadowlands."

Outside the cave of unforgiveness is a real world of sunlight, blue skies, and fresh air—the land of the living. But the prisoners in the cave do not believe it exists. Even when they are told over and over again that it does exist, they remain convinced their shadowland is the only world available to them.

So how do these prisoners break free from their shadowland and join the world of fresh air, radiant sunlight, soaring trees, and colorful flowers? How do they find life beyond the shadows? What if someone were to enter their shadowland, a person from the land of the living, and simply bring them to this better place?

As followers of Christ, this is the invitation extended to us in the act of forgiveness. By accepting the sacrifice for our sins on the cross by our Lord and Savior Jesus Christ, we are free from our shadowlands. "How much more will the blood of Christ, who through the eternal Spirit offered himself without blemish to God, purify our conscience from dead works to serve the living God" (Hebrews 9:14, esv). When we do the hard work of forgiveness, we experience the Kingdom of God in the here and now. We set a prisoner free—our very selves—from the shadowlands, and we accept the gracious invitation to walk with God and others in the land of the living.

ESSENTIAL PRACTICES

PRAY

Share. Open your heart to God, sharing any questions and struggles about what it might mean for you to embrace forgiveness. Also share your hopes about how your life might change on the other side of forgiveness.

Ask. Identify what you need from God in order to turn toward the land of the living. Ask him to give you the desire and the strength to forgive others, to forgive yourself, and even to forgive God if necessary.

Listen. Listen with an open heart for God's promptings about anything that might be keeping you stuck in resentment, bitterness, or unforgiveness. Also listen as he reassures you of his protection and care.

ACT

- Complete the exercise described in "Identify Who You Need to Forgive" (pages 148–150).

- Journal your responses to the following questions.

  » Do you believe that your faith—what you believe about God—is evident in how you live your life?

  » Do you believe the gospel—that Jesus died on the cross to forgive you of your sins?

  » Do you harbor resentments and unforgiveness toward anyone?

» If so, how might you shift your perspective—to really trust the gospel message of unconditional love—so you can forgive as you have been forgiven?

ADJUST

Based on what you learned from taking action, what adjustments do you want to make? Consider any adjustments in thought, speech, or behavior that could help you move closer to forgiveness. Write them in your journal.

GET

Part 3

CALLED

SHAYNE

I cried only once. I was in Kenya with a group of "mom bloggers," or journalists, as we were often introduced. Ten women, mothers from all walks of American life, traveled to Kenya to report first-hand on what life is like for other mothers half a world away. Our goal was to blog, share our experiences, and raise awareness about the realities of extreme poverty, maternal health, access to education, and the HIV/AIDS situation in Africa. In five short days, we traveled, bumped and bruised, by airplane, bus, and foot, to remote compounds around Lake Victoria and to the urban slum of Kibera in Nairobi.

One afternoon, we took a break from the intense things we had seen and experienced by visiting Amani ya Juu, a fair-trade sewing co-op in central Nairobi that advocates for marginalized women and girls from all over Africa by training and equipping them. Women who have been abused or cast out find safety and a vocation at Amani. *Amani* means *peace*.

Amani is an oasis in the city. We pulled into the walled compound and found well-kept gardens, a small café, a lovely store carrying the items the women make, and a large building housing their sewing rooms, a warehouse of materials, a pleasant chapel, and offices. It was a beautiful day. The sun was bright and there was a soft breeze as we ambled around the gardens and enjoyed a tour of the operations.

We climbed stone stairs that led to a large room with a high ceiling and enormous windows that let in all the light. A soft breeze danced around the women, sewing machines, and piles of brightly colored fabric. About twenty women gathered to introduce themselves. We began going around the room simply saying our names and where we were from.

"I'm Rachel. I live in North Carolina in the United States."

"Faith. I come from Uganda."

"Mary. Zambia."

"I'm Elisa. I come from Denver, Colorado."

"Shayne. Chicago, USA."

"Victoria. I come from Burundi."

"Florence. Kenya."

We continued around our circle. There was energy, joy, and

enthusiasm as we smiled deeply at one another, shook hands, and connected.

"Beatrice. Congo."

Beatrice was dressed in a drab cotton top and a burgundy-brown wrap skirt that went to the floor. Her head was covered in a scarf that matched her skirt. She spoke so softly I could hardly hear her. She did not lift her eyes from the spot on the floor at which she was gazing, and her body did not move when she uttered her name. *Beatrice.*

In the time it took to speak her name, her unspeakable pain washed over me. I saw a woman standing across from me, but I did not see a spirit. I saw the living dead. The other women most certainly had stories to tell about reasons they found themselves at Amani. Yet I could see Beatrice's pain. I could feel it from twenty feet away.

All this before she then muttered the unthinkable. *Congo.*

The word "Congo" sent a snapshot of pain straight to my heart. I knew that the Democratic Republic of the Congo was considered one of the worst places on earth to be a woman. I whipped my head around to hide the involuntary tears that overtook me.

I had woken up years ago to the realities of extreme poverty, out-of-control disease, and gender inequality in the three-fourths world. I had traveled internationally, seen desperate situations for myself, and studied reports of what life is like for women in countries rated among the worst places to be a woman.

My heart pounded as I wondered what Beatrice had experienced. What had her experiences of the world told her about her life? To be such a young woman and to be carrying so much pain, to be the walking dead, I know is the result of abuse and violence, neglect, and ignorance.

These thoughts were unleashed in my mind and soul as I backed away from the circle of women. I retreated to a corner window to catch my breath and collect myself. I did not want to have a breakdown, but I felt one coming on. I tried in vain to push down the emotions, and tears streamed down my face. The familiar space inside my heart was breached—that place of pain and powerlessness, that place of resignation mixed with despair for the way the world is for many women.

This experience caused me to think more about what makes me sad or mad, which are often the things I'm passionate about. And it revealed to me what ignites the sacred, internal flame within that motivates me to make a difference in the world. I began to be aware of and pay attention to those moments that stir emotions in my heart and soul.

8

TAKE THE PULSE OF
YOUR PASSIONS

Pay attention to the things that bring a tear to your eye or a lump in your
throat because they are the signs that the holy is drawing near.

FREDERICK BUECHNER

Linda was a young woman when she married Lloyd Reeb, a real estate developer who would later become cofounder of the Halftime Institute. When her children came along a few years later, Linda happily embraced the role of stay-at-home mom.

As a young mom, Linda was involved in many activities. She volunteered as a room mom at her children's school, played in the church band, taught a Sunday school class, and hosted a church small group. She was active in churches, organizations, and projects, and she enjoyed it all. This season of life made her glad and brought her joy.

When her children were in high school, Linda knew a big shift was coming. With her empty nest season looming, several things she enjoyed were coming to an end. She said it felt like pearls falling off a string necklace one by one. The kids were getting ready to launch out on their own, Lloyd was working full time, and Linda knew it would soon be time for her to find a purpose and live out her calling in her second half.

But Linda had a secret. She didn't feel a passion for anything. Lloyd's passion and work was helping people discover their own passions, and he was a tremendous success at it. Linda could not relate, and the more she observed her husband's work, the deeper her spirits sank. She did not know how to assess new opportunities or how to think critically about what the purpose of her second half might be. She felt paralyzed.

YOUR PURPOSE AND PASSIONS

Your job at this stage of the halftime process is to fully embrace the truth of your Ephesians 2:10 calling: that God has good works he has prepared in advance for you to do. God's Son died on the cross for you, and your purpose is inextricably tied to God's character and his will for our world. *You exist for a reason.*

Theologian Walter Elwell offers a compelling description of purpose based on the meanings of the biblical words for purpose, which are *yaas* in Hebrew and *boule* in Greek.

> The verbal root of the Hebrew word for purpose means
> to give counsel, deliberate, purpose, or determine. In
> five passages where the noun appears, four refer to God's
> purpose and one to the purpose of a person's heart
> (Proverbs 19:21; 20:5; Isaiah 46:10-11; Jeremiah 32:19).
> God's plans stand firm forever (Psalm 33:11); his purpose
> will stand (Isaiah 46:10). . . . He has a goal in what
> he does. Nothing can thwart his plan. His purpose is
> consistently related to what he does in the world. . . .

[In the New Testament] Paul understands that the
believer's part in the people of God is not an accident
or random phenomenon, but part of the divine purpose
from the very beginning of time (Romans 8:28-29).
God's purpose is specifically characterized by the words
"foreknew" and "predestined."

The good pleasure that God purposed in Christ has
now been put into effect and will be seen in its completion
when he sums up all things in Christ. In the meantime,
however, God has called his people to live a holy life
because of his own purpose and grace given before the
beginning of time in Christ Jesus, but now revealed in the
Savior's appearing.[1]

These truths about God's character and his purpose include
you. He has a goal in what he does in your life, and nothing can
thwart his plans for you.

You are at the point of your halftime journey where you have
done the hard work of getting clear on who you are and who you
are not. You understand that your identity, grounded in Christ,
will never change even though your circumstances may change.
You have worked to get free from fears and limiting beliefs that
get in the way of the wide-open spaces God calls you to in your
second half. Now you are at the Getting Called stage, where you
will go deeper and begin to fine-tune what your Ephesians 2:10
calling will look like.

Getting called to a purpose—the work God has prepared in
advance for you to do—requires getting a fresh perspective on
your passions. Passions are what motivate and inspire you. They
include the issues, causes, individuals, or groups of people that

energize you. Passions are what bring you to tears and what fire you up and get you out of bed in the morning. When you get called, your passions fuel your purpose. And as you explore your passions, you may discover that you are passionate about several things, all of which contribute to the unique purpose and mission God created just for you.

Your Passion Fuels Your Purpose

Christian philosopher Søren Kierkegaard said that the key to life is "to find the idea for which I am willing to live and die."[2] That's the essence of what a passion is. Passion is what fuels your dreams and informs your purpose.[3] Your passion gives you energy and joy; it is what calls you forward. Passion motivates you to explore new vistas, develop new relationships, and seek solutions to perplexing problems. Unfortunately, the challenge many women at midlife face is that, like Linda Reeb, they no longer have any idea what motivates them. Their passion has been buried under the responsibilities of caring for children, supporting elderly parents, and attending to the other demands in the first half of life.

There may be many things that interest you, but then there are those things that deeply move you and stir up energy, joy, or even anger in you. These passions are the things that keep you awake at night. The intensity of your emotions—of what makes you mad, sad, and glad—are all clues to your passion and purpose.

As Linda Reeb worked with a coach to navigate her transition from full-time mother to her second half, something began to happen within her heart. She observed the difficulties experienced by families she knew, and an emotion began to flicker within, a possible clue to her passion. Linda did her halftime work, including identifying her spiritual gifts and her strengths. Her findings all pointed her toward a calling in teaching, mentoring, and shepherding.

During this time, Linda was coached to reflect on her life and to recall what had brought her joy and made her glad in her first half. She realized that what had brought her the most joy was working with children and families, both her own and others. And she was delighted to discover that what had brought her the most gladness in the past was pointing her to her passions in the present.

As Linda was awakening to her hidden passions and seeking a new purpose, she also had a front-row seat to observe the lives of several families who were going through incredibly difficult times, including four friends in the midst of heartbreaking divorces. These situations grieved her. She realized that in addition to paying attention to what made her glad, she also needed to pay attention to what made her sad. She was beginning to understand that her emotions could be clues to what she was passionate about and to her life's purpose.

Linda discovered that what made her sad and mad were even more powerful indicators of her passions than the things that made her glad. She was devastated when her close friends lost their marriages to divorce. All of them were Christians and had young children. She often thought about what had gone wrong and how things might have been different for them and for other Christian families she saw breaking apart. When Linda's passion began to fuel her purpose, she couldn't shake thoughts like these: *What would it look like to minister to hurting women and hurting families? To be a conduit for God by mentoring and ministering to young moms? What about reaching out to moms at the beginning of family life instead of relying on therapists when things fall apart? What about helping mothers build strong foundations from the start?*

RESIST THE COMPARISON TRAP

CAROLYN

It is important to note that one passion is not better than another. While some women feel passionate about global causes, other women are passionate about local causes. Some creative souls find their passion in cooking, art, music, or cinema. Others find their passion and calling working with children, the elderly, or prisoners, or by contributing in the marketplace.

As you explore your passions, resist the unhealthy trap of comparison. Instead, cultivate contentment and grace. Just because someone else feels passionate about a certain cause doesn't mean that you need to.

I experienced the lure of the comparison trap when my halftime mentor founded an organization called Stop Hunger Now. He was deeply passionate about solving world hunger. While I certainly cared about world hunger, I cared about other things too. I had to resist the guilt I felt because this wasn't also my passion. Just because my mentor felt passionate about this cause didn't mean I needed to feel that passion on the same level he did.

When God places a call on your life, he has not called you to fulfill someone else's passion and calling. It's not helpful to look at the woman next to you and wonder, *Why don't I feel passionate about the same things she does?* Instead, focus on what God has uniquely called you to. Being honest with yourself about what fuels your passions and creates energy for your new purpose will lead you to your future.

As Linda used her passions to fuel her purpose, she went on to create her own ministry, which she called MomsMentoring. Today, Linda and her ministry encourage women to apply the wisdom of the Bible to their everyday lives, helping them to build strong marriages and Christian families.

Your Passion Isn't Necessarily Just One Thing

A common misconception about passions and purpose is that you must find that *one thing* you are wired to do. But what if your passions and your calling center around several issues or causes rather than just one?

Many women we coach feel frustrated when they cannot find one cause they feel passionate about. Some conclude they must be coldhearted or emotionally stunted in some way, as if their passions are a thing of the past. But there is another way to think about passions, and that is that your greatest joy and service may have less to do with a cause and more to do with who you were created to be, what God has prepared for you, and what you bring to the cause.

Investigative journalist David Epstein addresses this concept in his book *Range* when he describes individuals who are "generalists" in a specialized world. He discovered that in most fields, especially those that are complex and unpredictable, generalists are equipped to excel. Generalists, he maintains, often find their path late in life, and they juggle many interests rather than focusing only on one. They are creative and agile, and can make connections their more specialized peers do not notice. With the description of generalists, Epstein might well have been writing about a woman named Lisa Payne.

For twenty years, Lisa excelled in the business world, first as a vice president at Goldman Sachs, and then as vice chairman and chief financial officer at an international real estate investment trust. She also served on the investment trust's board of directors. A natural leader and achiever, Lisa thrived in the busyness of her professional life.

Like many women, Lisa began her halftime journey as her daughters were leaving the nest and she decided to retire from her high-powered position. With no office job to occupy her time and energy, Lisa struggled with what felt like terrifying hours of empty time. Her biggest challenge going into her second half was losing the busyness that had once filled her life. She excelled in and was wired for full and productive days. But now she was filled with fear about what might be ahead. How could she function in the world without a career?

"I thrived on busyness," Lisa reflects. "I now realize that part of that was because it kept me from having to go deep spiritually. Busyness, to me, was a purpose. I thrived in the business world for twenty years. Busyness seemed fulfilling because I didn't have time to think. But when I hit this season, I was suddenly overwhelmed with all the insecurity that came with wondering how I would find a new purpose as my old purpose was going away. That was my biggest challenge."

Motivated by her uncertainty and fears, Lisa immediately took another job. She was determined to do anything to keep her midlife fears at bay. Not surprisingly, this job did not work out and left Lisa with a choice: to continue chasing busyness or to look within herself and to God for guidance.

Lisa chose to look within by getting coaching and joining a cohort, a group of peers, both men and women, in the same season of life. Along with the others, she took tests to evaluate her strengths and spiritual gifts. She also did Enneagram work, a popular assessment of personality, motivations, and giftings. It was not a surprise when her Enneagram results indicated she was an Eight, often referred to as "the Challenger."

Lisa both laughed and cried when she read the description of her personality as powerful, dominating, self-confident, and willful. The results of the Enneagram assessment also described her as confrontational, a trait she readily owned. And her tough persona also masked a soft, vulnerable heart. The Challenger in her was always chasing something, but the deeper motives beneath the chase were feelings of fear and unworthiness. The cohort Lisa joined proved invaluable in dealing with the transitional phase of her life.

Lisa realized she had a misconception about her halftime process: She had thought there was a silver bullet to finding her calling. But she learned that calling doesn't work that way. Rather, it was her willingness to be authentic and having a community that allowed her to be vulnerable that proved most helpful in finding her calling. Having a community gave her a safe place to put into words what she was feeling inside.

Through monthly coaching sessions and quarterly cohort meetings Lisa discovered a vision for her second half. And just as she couldn't have chosen to focus on just one of her children, Lisa realized that she couldn't choose to focus on just one of her passions. In fact, living into her calling meant she must focus on all three of her passions, which were evangelism, opposing human trafficking, and working to end poverty, particularly helping women living in extreme poverty.

Once Lisa was clear on her passions, she felt that familiar buzz of accomplishment at having a new challenge. She finally had clarity about her passions and was eager to share them with her cohort.

In Lisa's prophetic imagination, she saw these three passions as the pillars that would uphold her next season. Her new multifaceted focus freed Lisa from both the insecurity of doing nothing meaningful and the fears that had driven her to pursue activities for the sake of busyness.

Pursuing her three passions opened many relationships and opportunities for Lisa to serve, give back, and use all of her Enneagram Eight superpowers.

There are many ways to reignite passions at midlife and find a purpose. Some women know immediately what they care deeply about, and they know what their dreams for their second-half purpose could look like. For them, the challenge is in executing them. For others, the challenge is making a connection between their emotions and their passions to begin with. Whatever your challenge may be, know that, as it was for Lisa, your passions might be lived out in more than one way.

TAKE THE PULSE OF YOUR MAD, SAD, GLAD

Like many women we've coached, Linda Reeb discovered her passions and purpose by paying attention to what made her mad, sad, and glad, and she now uses this approach to help those she mentors. She calls it taking one's emotional pulse. Taking her own emotional pulse ultimately took her way outside of her comfort zone to create a new ministry that fills her with joy and purpose. Linda's calling is to help young women attend to their emotional pulse while building a marriage, raising children, and then preparing for what they'll do when those babies leave home. Her goal is that no woman will feel overwhelmed by life's challenges, and that they will be prepared for the big transitions of life because they will already know their passions, purpose, and calling. The exercise that follows includes the questions Linda uses to assist women in taking the pulse of their mad, sad, and glad.

The goal of this exercise is to help you discern what your passions are today. Even if you feel like you already have a sense of what makes you mad, sad, and glad, engaging these questions will help you to determine if anything has changed.

Find a quiet spot, free from distractions, and journal your honest responses to the questions that follow. An alternative would be to work through the questions in conversation with a close friend or mentor. If you do that, be sure to record the conversation so you can listen to it and transcribe it for later reference.

"I studied myself and identified my strengths, gifts, passion, and calling. I recognized my hurts and failures were what God had used to draw me into a closer relationship with him."

Chris Travelstead, Halftime Institute board member

You may be surprised by what is revealed in the ebb and flow of an intimate conversation around what makes you mad, sad, and glad. All of it contains clues to your passions. The important part is to be honest and free of self-judgment and comparison.

- *What makes you glad?* Recall whatever makes your heart sing, inspires you to laugh, brings you the greatest joy, and makes you feel truly alive.

- *What makes you sad?* Consider what makes you cry and the needs that break your heart.

- *What makes you mad?* Focus on the causes, injustices, and issues that get you fired up.

- *What do you frequently think about, talk about, or read about out of desire and fascination?* Without effort, reflect on what you are drawn to and care about.

- *Who do you feel most called to serve?* Focus on the age group, community, demographics, or nationality of people you often think about.

After completing the exercise, reflect on what was harvested from your heart and mind about what inspires you, what you care about, and what raises these emotions in you. Is there anything that surprises you? Scares you? Challenges you? Excites you? Bring these things to the Lord in prayer.

CLEAR CALLING

In his bestselling book *The Purpose Driven Life*, Rick Warren writes, "God is not haphazard; he planned it all with great precision."[4] Reigniting the passions that fuel your purpose does not have to be overwhelming or mysterious. God has already planned good works, a good purpose, and a mission for your life. Your job is to trust God. He is always faithful. As you work through the stage of Getting Called, remember you are his child. He knew you in your mother's womb, and he came to give you life and give it abundantly. A numb, dull, directionless second half is not his will for anyone. As you awaken to your passions and fuel your purpose, and as you hone in on what your calling might be, lean into God and his Word. Your calling will reflect who God is, who he made you to be, and what his will is for your life. The more you learn the character and the heart of God, the clearer your calling will become.

ESSENTIAL PRACTICES

PRAY

Share. Talk with God about what makes you mad, sad, and glad.

Ask. Ask God to assist you in understanding and recognizing how your emotions—what surprises you, scares you, or excites you— might reveal details about your passions and your calling.

Listen. Listen for the Lord's guidance, reassurance, and presence as you identify your passions in order to serve him.

ACT

- Complete the exercise in "Take the Pulse of Your Mad, Sad, Glad" (pages 168–170).

- Choose one of the issues you identified that make you mad, sad, or glad and brainstorm three to five ways you could take a step toward that issue. A step might be anything from learning more about the issue to identifying organizations that work in that area and searching out volunteer opportunities. Choose one idea and follow through on it within the next week.

ADJUST

Based on what you've learned about what makes you mad, sad, and glad, or on what you have learned about the character of God, what adjustments do you want to make to reignite your passions? Consider any adjustments in thought, speech, or behavior that could help you move forward. Write them in your journal.

DISCOVER WHAT FITS YOU

Then I heard the voice of the Lord, saying, "Whom shall I send,
and who will go for Us?" Then I said, "Here am I. Send me!"

ISAIAH 6:8, NASB

Like many women at midlife, Rhonda Kehlbeck was filled with
conflicting emotions as her youngest daughter was about to leave
for college. While she was excited about the prospect of pursuing
a joy-filled second half, she also felt confused and overwhelmed
nearly every day. For decades, she had taken care of her family and
never even thought of what she might be passionate about or what
direction she might go in her second half. She felt a prayer welling
up inside her, saying, "Here I am, Lord, send me," but had no idea
where that prayer might take her.

Rhonda felt sadness because she had loved being a mom and
felt she had done an excellent job of it. It was a role in which she
felt needed. How could her next season be better than the rewards
of raising her two girls? Even though she had a PhD in education,

had been a part-time professor at a university and a speaker for MOPS, and even written a book for parents, Rhonda felt professionally unqualified. She had been out of the full-time workforce for twenty years. The thought of getting out there and looking for her calling, her next job, was terrifying. Who would hire someone who hadn't worked full-time for two decades? Even more, what would fit her in this next season of life after her first half was centered around the needs of her family? She felt ill-equipped to discover what fit her now.

TAKE A TEST-DRIVE

In the first half of life, many of us are driven by the need to provide, to achieve, to establish ourselves. We may have had a family to care for and now have a career to launch, a life to make. As children approach adulthood themselves or our professional lives change, we might feel ready and even eager to get going in our second half, but the question is, where? What fits our lives now when so much of what we built our lives around in our first half is changing?

We've said it before, but it bears repeating. When faced with life-changing challenges or significant transitions, the temptation is to immediately jump to the next thing, to replace uncertainty with certainty by making a commitment to whatever presents itself first. The problem is that making a premature commitment short-circuits an essential component of halftime, which is taking time

> *"Clarity on my core and confidence in my capacity led to some interesting test-drives that helped me narrow down where God was guiding me next."*
>
> Nancy Lopez, leadership and career transition coach

to explore options. We often refer to exploring options as taking a test-drive, or multiple test-drives, so you can live out who you are (and who you are not) in short-term ways before making a long-term commitment.[1] You might also call it a try-before-you-buy or a date-before-you-marry approach; just don't call it a long-term commitment yet.

In fact, if we could give you just one gift, it would be the gift of time to try out new things without the pressure of making a long-term commitment. Taking a few test-drives enables you to practice the emotional intelligence competency of emotional reasoning. Emotional reasoning is what allows you to use your emotions to make good decisions. It's also what enables you to embrace the things that don't work out as "lessons" rather than "failure." Taking test-drives is essential because you can't merely think your way into good decisions in your second half. Instead, just as you did in your first half, you must fully engage life and make decisions based on what you learn from hands-on experience. To do that, you need to get behind the wheel, make God your copilot, and expect him to make divine connections.

Get Behind the Wheel

Getting behind the wheel means mustering the courage to act on all of your hard work thus far. Imagine you are about to buy a new car you plan to keep for the next ten years. Most likely, you would want to get behind the wheel to make sure the seating is comfortable, and then check how the car feels as you drive it. Before you invest your money, you want to know if the car fits you and feels good. The goal of getting behind the wheel for your next season is to make a short-term commitment to a job or volunteer position that aligns well with your strengths, talents, values, and passions.

Here are some guidelines to help you get behind the wheel.

Be a proactive communicator. Make it clear from the start that you are looking for a trial period. Ask for a clearly defined role, a set number of hours per day or week, and a specific time period (usually a few weeks or months). Ask questions to make sure you're clear on what your potential supervisor or the organization as a whole needs from you. In fact, depending on the role, it's always good to establish the metrics of success. Ask your contact person, "What will define success for my time here?" Then ask clarifying questions until you're clear on what success looks like for both you and the organization.

Establishing clarity before you begin allows for a graceful exit strategy if you find this role is either not a good fit for you or that you want to take more test-drives before you commit. When you communicate your boundaries up front, it's less likely there will be hard feelings or misunderstandings later. It also helps to alleviate the fear of commitment because there is no commitment, only a short-term learning opportunity.

Document your experience. Use your journal to document your observations, emotions, and experiences along the way. Remember, your goal is to be a student of your own life and experiences when you get behind the wheel. When you document what you notice and learn about yourself, you're gathering essential data to help you make intentional and informed decisions in the future.

Think of it as an adventure. Rhonda decided she was up for an adventure and looked for an opportunity to plug in where she saw God was already working. Wanting to make the most of her degrees and experience in education, she started by volunteering at a small Christian school that served students living below poverty level. When a kindergarten teacher unexpectedly resigned two months later, the school asked Rhonda if she would be interested in taking over the class. Even though she had previously taught only graduate students, Rhonda jumped at the chance to take a seven-month test-drive.

"How hard can it be to teach kindergartners?" she reasoned.

The answer: a lot harder than she thought! And yet, Rhonda was up for the adventure of whatever God wanted to teach her. "When I told God, 'Here I am, ready for you to tell me what I should do,' God knew I wasn't yet ready for my calling," she said. "He needed to work on me first, prune me, and shape me into the person I needed to be to find my sweet spot. I clearly needed a lot of work because he sent me all the way back to kindergarten!"

There is no such thing as adventure without mishaps along the way—that's just part of the package. Having a sense of humor about it helps, as does keeping the big picture in mind—everything you experience is a lesson that gets you one step closer to your best fit.

Make God Your Copilot

Rhonda was less than two hours into her first day as a kindergarten teacher when she reached her wit's end. She had tried every teacher trick she knew, but the room was in chaos, and she was ready to quit. "Lord, I can't handle this," she prayed. "Unless you come down here and do something, I'm leaving at noon, and I'm not coming back."

A few minutes later, the classroom door opened and in walked the school janitor, Mr. Jackson. Without saying a word, he walked over and gave Rhonda a hug. Then he turned and quietly walked out of the room. That small gesture of compassion helped her make it through the rest of the day without quitting.

The next day she asked him, "Why did you come into my room and give me a hug yesterday?"

He smiled and said, "I try and live so close to the Holy Spirit that when he says, 'Get in there, she needs you,' I go in."

Rhonda was moved. She wanted that kind of relationship with the Lord, to live so attuned to the Holy Spirit that she could hear his every whisper, even amidst chaos. She wanted God to be her copilot, to talk with her and lead her as he did Mr. Jackson. And the truth was, Rhonda was desperate. She needed God's help every minute of every day in that classroom. Rhonda started getting up early each day to spend time with God because she wanted to be as close to him as she could. And that's when the miracles started happening.

During her first few weeks of teaching, Rhonda became concerned about one of her students. Brandon couldn't focus, and his behavior was disruptive. She had a feeling he had learning differences and needed more help than she could give. When she shared her concerns with the elementary school headmistress, the woman affirmed Rhonda's concerns but said that her hands were tied. "The school can't afford to pay for him to be tested," she said, "and testing agencies are no longer offering scholarships." Rhonda's own daughter had learning differences, and she couldn't imagine Brandon not getting the help he needed. Without giving it a second thought, Rhonda said, "I'll pay for his testing." The headmistress said, "Okay, but it will probably cost $1,500 to $2,000, and they'll ask for a $275 deposit to reserve his initial appointment." Rhonda immediately wrote out a check.

The following Sunday, Rhonda was teaching her Sunday school class, a group of women between seventy and a hundred years of age. Each week, these women asked Rhonda for an update on how her teaching stint was going. Before teaching her lesson, she briefly told them about the student who needed educational testing but couldn't afford it. She didn't tell them she had planned to pay for it. She simply asked them to pray.

In the middle of her lesson, one of the women sitting on the back row stood up and announced, "The ladies in my row have all agreed that we're donating to Brandon's testing. We're each giving $200." She then proceeded to ask all the other women in the class to donate. Before Rhonda knew it, she had collected $1,475 in cash. When she got to school the following day, she went straight to the headmistress to find out if she had learned the cost of Brandon's testing.

"The total will be $1,750," she said. Rhonda had already given $275 to secure Brandon's testing appointment, so with the $1,475 from the women in her class, she had $1,750 exactly. "Crazy miraculous!" Rhonda exclaimed. Brandon was assessed for learning differences by the leading educational testing facility, also a school, in Dallas. His test results showed that he did indeed have severe learning differences and needed extra help to succeed in life. As a result, the leaders at the school that tested Brandon took action. As Rhonda puts it, the outcome was nothing short of a miracle. The testing school gave him a full-ride scholarship of $18,000 because administrators knew how much Brandon needed their help. He continued to excel there year after year.

As Rhonda learned, and you likely will, too, you are never alone when you make God your test-drive copilot. When you press into the power, resources, and creativity of the One who knows your best path forward, he will lead and empower you during this trial period. And you may even experience some miracles along the way, as Rhonda did. Your path will not always be easy, but you can take comfort in knowing that you don't have to take this test-drive solo. You have a copilot who already knows the way.

Expect God to Make Divine Connections

As challenging as it was, Rhonda stuck with her kindergarten test-drive. By the end of the school year, however, she felt sure God didn't intend for her to continue when working with five-year-olds sucked the life out of her. Exhausted and somewhat confused, Rhonda decided to take a step back and work with a coach for a while to consider her options. Although she didn't know it at the time, God was already at work making divine connections on her behalf.

During the time she was working with her coach, the CEO of the Halftime Institute asked Rhonda if she would be willing to help other people at midlife find their Ephesians 2:10 calling. It was a role Rhonda would never have imagined for herself. When the institute created a job tailor-made for her passions, she felt as if God were using every one of her first-half experiences and skills in a new and creative way.

Today, Rhonda refers to her kindergarten test-drive as her season in the wilderness. At first, she wanted to get out of it as fast as she could. But she soon learned not to rush the desert experience. God was preparing her for her sweet spot—teaching her what it meant to trust him completely and allowing her to see miracles she describes as "so outrageous" that there was no doubt God was up to something. But God was still at work, making even more divine connections.

A year later, a Halftime Institute board member introduced Rhonda to her wealth manager. The manager told Rhonda about one of his clients who wanted to be more intentional about her next season of life. When his client said she wanted to give a large donation to a school that served underprivileged kids, the wealth manager contacted four schools for the donor to consider. The client met with the headmaster of each school and asked each one to share their success numbers. The final interview was with the principal of West Dallas Community School, where Rhonda had taught. When the client asked the headmaster about the school's success numbers, he said, "We don't have huge success numbers, but we do have miracles happening at our school." He then told her about a young boy named Brandon and the miraculous changes that had happened in his life after he'd been tested.

"I want to give my money to a school where miracles are happening," the donor said. And then she gave Brandon's school a $500,000 donation. The donor had no idea Rhonda had previously worked at the school or that she had been Brandon's teacher. Rhonda said, "It was such a gift that God allowed me to know, one year later, that the miracles he allowed me to be part of there were continuing."

Like Rhonda, you may not yet be able to see all the divine connections God is already making on your behalf. Most likely, you will face a few blind curves along your road or turn down a few dead ends. But even there, when you open your eyes to the possibility of miracles on the journey, you can rely on this promise: "God causes all things to work together for good to those who love God, to those who are called according to His purpose" (Romans 8:28, NASB). Your calling will require you to lean in and lean on God more than ever. His places and platforms for you are sweeter and more significant than anything you could come up with on your own.

If there's one thing we have learned over the years of coaching women through the test-drive stage of halftime, it's that God's purposes, as well as his miracles, will become evident along the journey. And perhaps the greatest miracle of all is the transformation women experience as they open their minds and hearts to God's possibilities for their future.

THE POWER OF "WHAT IF?"

At this stage of the halftime journey, we encourage the women we coach to embrace what we call the power of "What if?" It's a simple question, but it has the power to reignite your dreams. When you ask, "What if?" you switch your focus from what you lack to what is possible. It's a shift from a scarcity mentality to an abundance mentality.

There is no doubt that investing the time and effort required to take test-drives for your life comes with risks. But if your copilot is the God of all abundance, you can ask some empowering what-if questions. For example, what if his calling on your life could be fun? What if you stop limiting yourself? What if you can muster the courage to take just one step? What if you crushed any lies holding you back? We have witnessed in hundreds of lives that tremendous possibility begins with two small words that ask one big question: *What if?*

> *"I tried to find the box I fit in, but there never was one, and I came to be okay with that."*
>
> Barbara Mulkey, *former director of the Shelton Leadership Center*

One of the best examples we know that demonstrates the power of "What if?" is the story of Michelle Spadafora. Michelle and her husband, Jeff, both came to faith later in life. When the truth of the gospel and God's love for her and her family transformed her soul, Michelle wanted her life to serve a larger purpose, to feel that she was making an eternal impact. At the time,

Michelle led an award-winning event-planning business. However, despite the success and accolades, Michelle felt discontent and unfulfilled. Michelle explains, "There was no meaning attached to it anymore." And so she began to ask the what-if questions.

What If Your Calling Can Be Fun?

The question of whether her calling could be fun was actually an easy one for Michelle. She had already built a successful business around creating fun events, and she loved celebrating life. She wanted to make an eternal impact with her life, but she didn't want to limit herself to what other people were already doing. She committed herself to being creative and to making her second half exciting. Michelle wanted to dive headfirst into finding her Ephesians 2:10 calling with the new and profound belief that she was God's workmanship, and he had prepared a place for her.

When Michelle began to explore new places and platforms, she consulted friends who knew her well and understood her passions. Finally, one friend blurted it out, plain and simple: "Michelle, your calling is with faith, fitness, and food."

It was like a light bulb switched on.

"You're right!" she said. "That's what I'm created to do—faith, fitness, food."

So often when a woman considers her second-half calling, she tends to limit her perspective to something that sounds super spiritual, very serious, or even difficult. While that may indeed be the path to which God calls you, there's also the possibility that it's not.

What if your calling could be fun? What possibilities open up when you think about devoting your second half to something enjoyable?

What If You Stop Limiting Yourself?

Michelle's wheels were spinning with possibilities, but she did not know where to start. This idea about her calling was totally new. She had worked as a fitness trainer and had been cooking her whole life, but how was she supposed to combine fitness and food with faith? It seemed impossible to fit all three together in a meaningful way.

Michelle realized that she was limiting her thinking about how God could use her and wondered how her thoughts might change if she asked more what-if questions.

What if I stop limiting myself?

What if I don't let finances limit me?

What if I don't let my insecurities and my fears limit me?

What if I just go to God and say, "Here I am, send me. What is it you have for me?"

Because Michelle had come to faith later in life, she had a heart for people like herself who had never heard the message of Christ. Where Michelle lived, only 7 percent of the population were church attenders. Michelle lifted this concern and her heart for others to God. As she prayed, she realized that she had placed a limit on her thinking by focusing primarily on the impossibility of trying to get unchurched people into church. When she let go of that limitation, another light bulb lit up. If she couldn't get people into church to hear the gospel, she would bring the gospel to people through a fitness platform. That's how she could combine fitness and food with faith.

What if you stop limiting yourself? What possibilities could open when you set aside the limitations that keep you from pursuing the dreams you have for your second half?

What If You Take Just One Step?

When Michelle asked, "What if I take just one step?" she started by focusing on what was right in front of her. At the time, she was teaching a fitness class at a local health club and decided her first step would be to incorporate some Christian music into her classes. When Michelle's class became very popular, a mentor suggested she take this unique platform for reaching unchurched people through fitness and pitch it to cable television producers at an upcoming National Religious Broadcasters convention. Michelle was excited by this opportunity and embraced it. The night before she flew out to the convention in Nashville, she made a demo she describes as the cheesiest spur-of-the-moment workout video ever.

"When I got to the convention, I felt lost," Michelle recalls. "It seemed like everybody knew everybody else, and I was sitting there feeling so awkward and uncomfortable. I thought, *What am I doing here? I don't know anyone. What am I supposed to do? Say, "Hey, you, here's a DVD of my idea for a Christian exercise show?"*

Michelle was way out of her comfort zone trying to find her fit and sell her idea. And yet, she had taken not just one step, but a series of first steps. And her story wasn't over yet.

What if you take just one step? Even though it might be well outside your comfort zone, what one step could you take in the direction of your dreams?

What If You Crush the Lies Holding You Back?

One week after Michelle returned home from the conference, she received a call offering her a spot on DirecTV for a Christian exercise show that would air five mornings a week. Michelle was ecstatic! But then she began to hear the lying voices of her limiting beliefs. *You are nobody. Who wants to watch a forty-seven-year-old work out? You are too old. And what do you have to say about faith, fitness, and food?*

Fortunately, she also heard the voice of truth. She felt God saying, *"Don't you dare listen to those lies. Crush them. This is what I created you to do. Go and do it!"*

Michelle had a choice to make—to listen to the lies or to crush them and get moving. She chose to crush the lies and then watched God perform miracle after miracle. He provided financing to make the shows and the right production team to film them. Less than a year after getting her offer, Michelle kicked off *Faithful Workouts* on DirecTV.

After celebrating eleven years on the network, Michelle also started a new show called *The Fresh Table*. The show is devoted to empowering viewers to make healthy changes in the way they cook. When she had doubts about how to incorporate her faith with fitness and food, she sensed God's voice of truth saying to her, *"You are the messenger. I will give you the message."* And he does for every show.

In everything she does, Michelle is living out her calling to help people become healthy and whole in body, mind, and spirit. Through multiple platforms, including a website with a large membership, she brings her viewers joy and helps them to discover God in a fun way. People have reached out, sometimes depressed or even suicidal, to let her know that they somehow found her show and were helped and encouraged by it. From the first steps Michelle took to explore her calling, she felt God wanted her to be authentic; he didn't want her to pretend that she had it all together. And so, part of her calling has always been to encourage people to take off their masks. By having the courage to be who she was created to be, she gives others permission to do the same.

What if you crush the lies holding you back? How might your second half be different if you embrace the message God spoke to Michelle: "This is what I created you to do. Go and do it"?

As you open your mind to new possibilities and pursue your dreams, chances are that you will have to crush lies and limiting beliefs more often than you'd like. But what if you embrace the power of the what-if questions in this next season? What if you decide to have fun with your Ephesians 2:10 calling and the test-drives you take along the way? What if you stop limiting yourself and open your eyes to the miracles of the journey? What if you dare to take one step, knowing you have a copilot always holding your hand and working all things for your good? What if you crush the lies holding you back? *What if?*

DESIGN THREE TEST-DRIVES

In chapter 6, Create Capacity for Your New Path Forward, we encouraged you to identify three possible paths forward and to estimate the capacity you might need for each option. Now it's time to take the next step by identifying one test-drive for each of those ideas. You might think about it as you would if you were planning a road trip, identifying your destination and everything you'll need to do to get there.

The essential components of planning a meaningful test-drive for your second half include identifying four things:

- *A desired role.* A desired role is the part you want to play—one aligned with your strengths, talents, values, and passions. For example, do you want to be a team leader or a team member? Do you want to be a spokesperson or a behind-the-scenes person? Do you want to be a social entrepreneur or an executive?

Your role may change over time, and we will unpack that possibility more in part 4: Get Going. For now, think about what you want your role and responsibilities to be.

- *A desired outcome.* Outcomes are the results you hope to achieve from this test-drive. What do you hope will have happened by the end of your trial period? Note that you might have more than one desired outcome. You might want to learn something about yourself, learn something about the organization, or learn something about a cause. For example, a potential desired outcome of volunteering at a food bank might be to get involved in feeding hungry families in your community, learning if you fit with the culture of the organization, and discerning whether you are in the flow of God's will. The potential desired outcomes of leading a women's Bible study might be to strengthen and encourage the women in your church or to discover if you thrive in the role of leader. The desired outcomes of being a consultant might be to help ministries or companies solve specific challenges, and to discern if you want to be in one place full-time or if you love the challenge of working with many different organizations.

  When we coach women, we never choose an outcome for them. What you hope to achieve is entirely up to you. Determine what is most important for you to learn, both personally and about a particular organization or cause. These are just ideas to get you started. What outcomes do you hope to achieve on this test-drive?

- *A time commitment.* Your time commitment is the number of hours per day or week you can commit. Would you like this test-drive to be full-time, or just a few hours or days per week? It's important to determine this before contacting any prospective ministries or organizations. How much time are you able to give to this test-drive?

- *A graceful exit strategy.* An exit strategy is a clearly defined and agreed-upon ending point. It includes both a date on which the test-drive ends and clear communication that this is a temporary commitment. You'll save yourself many misunderstandings by telling people up front that you want to consider several paths forward before you commit. On what date will your test-drive end? What other factors, if any, will help you to gracefully exit this test-drive?

Briefly refer back to the three paths forward you identified in chapter 6 (pages 130–132). If you recall, we suggest that one might be the path you are currently on. Another might be a one- or two-degree shift, and the third might be a reach path. For this exercise, feel free to use the same three paths you identified in chapter 6, or use new options if your thinking has changed. The following charts demonstrate how our coaching client, the real estate broker from chapter 6, approached her test-drives.

Test-Drive 1: Continue as a real estate broker, my current path	
Desired Role	Continue to excel in my role as real estate broker. However, instead of resenting the hard work, I would approach each day with gratitude. I also want to be more intentional about helping my team to excel and to approach their work with gratitude as well.
Desired Outcome	My desired outcome is to build a firm financial foundation for my family and for retirement. This could provide a nest egg for future possibilities.

Time Commitment	I could give this path six more months while I pray, track how I feel, and document my desired role and outcome. Instead of 60–80 hours per week, I would also like to consider cutting back to 40–45 hours per week for a better work-life balance.
Graceful Exit Strategy	In six months, I will consider moving to Test-Drive 3 to reduce my hours even more and to create more time for ministry. While I take this test-drive, I will be intentional about blessing everyone in my path and keeping the doors open here. This strategy requires a meeting with my boss to explain that I will be cutting back to 40–45 hours a week for the next six months.

Test-Drive 2: Become a full-time speaker and author working in at-risk communities

Desired Role	A test-drive could be contacting my church and offering to lead a Bible study series on empowering women.
Desired Outcome	I want to give back to my community full-time, especially women, to let them know that God has greater plans for their lives. I want to test this out to see if I enjoy this work in a larger capacity.
Time Commitment	I will need at least one teaching opportunity a week for three months to test out my ideas for talks and to help me get a feel for this lifestyle versus the world of real estate. I will also need one or two days a week to develop teaching content, to write articles, and to pitch my ideas to magazines and blogs.
Graceful Exit Strategy	I need to have a clear conversation with the women's ministries director to let her know that I'm interested in just a three-month commitment for one night per week. Setting a firm date will give both of us clarity and avoid potential misunderstanding.

Test-Drive 3: Reduce hours in my real estate work to make time for ministry work

Desired Role	I would have two roles on a parallel track: real estate broker and speaker/writer. I would need to reach out to my church or to another ministry for a short-term test-drive teaching a Bible study series for women.

Desired Outcome	My desired outcome is to live my dream of giving back to my at-risk community, while continuing to provide for my family. As I process all of these paths, this one feels like a real possibility for the future, maybe after first trying Test-Drive 1.
Time Commitment	If I cut back my real estate work to 32 hours a week, I could give myself one day a week to fully develop my teaching material, lead an empowerment study series for women, and begin writing articles.
Graceful Exit Strategy	This exit strategy requires clear communication to both the women's ministries director and my boss, with a targeted end date. Letting my boss know that this is a temporary test-drive of 32 hours per week will provide clarity and keep the door open to returning to full-time work if this path ends up not being the right fit.

Now it's your turn. As you create three possible test-drives, think about the ministries and other organizations that might be a right fit for a temporary assignment. Pay special attention to how you feel and what your heart is telling you. You will only know if this is a good fit once you get behind the wheel and start driving.

Test-Drive 1:	
Desired Role	
Desired Outcome	

Time Commitment	
Graceful Exit Strategy	

Test-Drive 2:	
Desired Role	
Desired Outcome	
Time Commitment	
Graceful Exit Strategy	

Test-Drive 3:	
Desired Role	
Desired Outcome	
Time Commitment	
Graceful Exit Strategy	

As you review your three test-drive options, which one calls to your heart? Make that test-drive your focus and identify your next steps to pursue it. As you do, pay attention to any positive or negative emotions that come up for you. Note them and any other observations and insights you have in your journal.

After your test-drive is complete, use the list of statements on page 194 to assess your experience. Next to each statement, write down the number that best describes your response. Use the following scale:

5 = Strongly agree
4 = Agree
3 = Undecided
2 = Disagree
1 = Strongly disagree

Rating	Statement
	I was effective in this role.
	I am passionate about the activities I participated in.
	The purpose of this organization aligns with my values.
	I experienced the environment as life-giving.
	I developed positive relationships and felt affirmed by my colleagues.
	I felt there was a clear alignment between my role and my identity.
	I felt as if I were in the flow of my strengths, talents, and spiritual gifts.
	The activities brought me joy and a sense of purpose.
	The test-drive brought me peace that was beyond my comprehension.
	I can imagine a long-term commitment to this work or organization in the future.

If your responses are mostly 4s and 5s, this test-drive is likely a good fit for you. If your responses are mostly 1s and 2s, then this test-drive is likely not a good fit for you. Note any other observations you have about your test-drive experience in your journal.

Next, assess your test-drive from the perspective of capacity. Journal your responses to the following questions.

- *Time capacity.* How would a long-term role here fit with my available time?

- *Financial capacity.* How would a long-term role here affect my financial situation?

- *Mental capacity.* What impact would a long-term role here have on my emotional and mental well-being? What did my emotions tell me about this experience?

- *Spiritual capacity.* How would a long-term role here affect my spiritual health and growth?

Use everything you learn from assessing your experience to decide whether this is a good fit for you or if it's best to move on to another test-drive. And give yourself permission to have fun on this journey. Remember Michelle Spadafora's experience and keep the what-if questions front and center on your GPS as you take your test-drive. Be prepared for a few "recalculating" adjustments along the way. There is no failure on a test-drive, only new learning about what fits you in this season and what belongs in your rearview mirror.

THE SONG OF YOUR SOUL

Every good road trip needs a soundtrack. When it comes to charting the course for your second half, the tune you want to listen to most is the song of your soul. Turn the volume up high. Sing along with abandon. Have fun even as you adjust your route, make some turns, and adjust again. Test-drives are a gift and ultimately a time-saver—they save you from making a long-term commitment to a poor fit. Will you let the beautiful music play out in your life—your best life?

You need to keep the volume up on the song of your soul because that's what will keep you going as you navigate the twists and turns of finding what fits you best. Remember, there's no such thing as failure in halftime as long as you keep trying. That principle applies to test-drives as well. If you can learn to embrace the lessons of taking a test-drive that ends up being the wrong place, you'll still be one step closer to finding the right place. And you can be sure that God is still at work in making divine connections—and perhaps even miracles—on your behalf.

ESSENTIAL PRACTICES

PRAY

Share. Be open with God about your hopes and fears of taking a test-drive, and the adventure of possibly being in some wrong places before finding your best fit. Share your feelings with your copilot, who is on this journey with you.

Ask. Ask for the courage to have fun and to take some calculated risks for a short period of time. Pray for the courage to set clear boundaries for your test-drive.

Listen. Attune the ears of your heart to whispers of wisdom from God as you identify potential test-drives. Listen as he sings to you the song of your soul.

ACT

- Complete the three charts in "Design Three Test-Drives" (pages 191–193). Journal your responses to the following questions.

  » What thoughts and feelings are you aware of when you consider following through on at least one of these three short-term options for moving forward?

  » What would help you to see each test-drive as an opportunity for adventure?

  » What support or encouragement do you need to follow through on taking a test-drive?

- Choose one of the test-drives you identified and list two or three next steps you can take within the next seven to ten days to pursue it. Set deadlines and invite a friend to hold you accountable for taking each step.

- Journal your responses to the what-if questions at the end of each section in "The Power of What If?" (pages 183–187).

ADJUST

Based on what you've learned from taking action, what adjustments do you want to make? Consider any adjustments that would free up more time for taking a test-drive or enable you to have more fun taking a test-drive. Write them in your journal.

WRITE A PURPOSE STATEMENT

I coach, speak, and write to equip leaders for Christ.

CAROLYN CASTLEBERRY HUX

As a corporate director with McDonald's Corporation, Cheryl Hunter spent her career motivated and driven to succeed. However, as she approached her fiftieth birthday, she began to feel her career growth was limited at the corporate level and decided to try her hand at being an entrepreneur by franchising with McDonald's.

In addition to being a successful business owner, Cheryl had a lifelong love of children and families. At age twenty-five, she adopted a nine-month-old baby boy from Korea. She had her first biological child ten years later. While the business side of her life was thriving, Cheryl also fulfilled her passion of loving others and pouring into their lives. At the time she decided to leave her corporate job and become a business owner, Cheryl adopted a four-month-old baby girl from China. At church, her family met a twenty-year-old young man from Korea named Zac. Zac had been abandoned by his first adoptive family and was searching for belonging. Cheryl and her family often invited him to their home for dinner and holidays. As this relationship grew, Zac and Cheryl realized they were family. With Zac's background of abandonment and loss, formalizing their relationship was an important part of his healing. So at twenty-five, it became official and Zac was adopted.

For the next several years, Cheryl's life was full with building successful businesses and caring for her four children. In 2013, she decided to sell her franchises and then began to wonder, *What's next?* That's when she started working with a coach from Halftime Institute who helped her write a purpose statement for her second half of life. Instead of retiring, she wanted to use her special skill set to do the work God had for her in the next season of life.

Sadly, Cheryl's life took a tragic turn in 2018 when Zac, then thirty-nine, suffered complications after an unexpected heart surgery. His sudden death devastated the family. Even in her pain, Cheryl knew the mission God had given her and was able to use her suffering to minister to others. Finding purpose in both her work experience and her losses, Cheryl has devoted her life to connecting with others as she helps them find their purpose in business and in life.

WHAT IS A PURPOSE STATEMENT?
A purpose statement is a guide for your second half. It helps you decide what you will say yes to and what you will say no to. Crafting a purpose statement is powerful because it captures your calling, dreams, strengths, spiritual gifts, passions, values, and desired

context into one sentence. And this one sentence defines who you are, what you want, and what you intend to do with your life. It is the culmination of all the work you have done so far in this process.

A purpose statement is the personal version of a mission statement. Just as an organization or business relies on a good mission statement as the focus of its distinctive identity and success, you will rely on your purpose statement as you pursue fulfillment in your second half. The goal of a purpose statement is to focus on the big picture for your life, not to design every little detail for your next season. It is about listening carefully for the unique Ephesians 2:10 calling and assignment God has given you and having the courage to put it down in writing. Your purpose statement enables you to stay focused on what God is calling you to do. It helps you act on your dreams so you can get going and stay the course of God's agenda for your life.

As you prepare to craft your purpose statement, you may find it helpful to take cues from some strategic management experts. For example, here is how Peter Drucker, a renowned management consultant, educator, and author, describes the qualities of a good mission statement.

> The effective mission statement is short and sharply focused. It should fit on a T-shirt. The mission statement says *why* you do what you do, not the means by which you do it. The mission is broad, even eternal, yet directs you to the right things now and into the future. . . . It must be clear, and it must inspire.[1]

Note the point Drucker makes about the *why* of the statement versus the *means*. An effective purpose statement captures your ultimate objective rather than the strategy you'll use to reach your objective.

Fred R. David, an internationally recognized strategic planning scholar and author, summarizes a mission statement this way:

> Sometimes called a creed statement, a statement
> of purpose, a statement of philosophy, a statement
> of beliefs . . . a mission statement reveals what an
> organization wants to be and whom it wants to serve.[2]

We especially love that last line. In fact, one way to think about your purpose statement is to ask yourself, "Who do I want to be? Who do I want to serve?"

As we coach women through writing their purpose statement, we focus on four key characteristics. A good purpose statement is dynamic, concise, a guide, and cumulative.

A Purpose Statement Is Dynamic

Your purpose statement must be dynamic, meaning energetic and action oriented. Drawing on all the work you have done in your transformational change process, your purpose statement should create action in your life with the purpose of achieving your goal.

We opened this chapter with Carolyn's purpose statement: "I coach, speak, and write to equip leaders for Christ." Her purpose statement is dynamic because it states who Carolyn is, whom she serves, and the actions she takes to accomplish her goals.

A Purpose Statement Is Concise

A good purpose statement is short and to the point. In his classic book on writing, *The Elements of Style*, William Strunk states,

"When a sentence is made stronger, it usually becomes shorter. Thus, brevity is a by-product of vigor."[3] Vigor means to put forth effort, energy, and enthusiasm. Crafting a direct, focused, and short statement may take work and perhaps many drafts, but when you're done, you will have a strong and concise statement to guide your second half.

"I'm living my purpose statement and teaching a class for young communicators to go and influence their generation. I have a goal of empowering 100,000 women in their story so they can share it with others for Jesus Christ and his Kingdom."

Tracey Lynn Russell, host of The Heart of the Story *podcast*

Here are a couple of examples to consider. The mission statement for Target is concise and to the point: "To help all families discover the joy of everyday life." The mission statement for the Christian humanitarian organization World Relief is to "empower the local church to serve the most vulnerable." These are great examples of how a purpose statement can be both short and effective.

A Purpose Statement Is a Guide

As you embark on the Get Going season of halftime, you will not be able to say yes to everything that excites you, captures your imagination, or interests you. That's why it is essential to have boundaries that help you decide what to say yes to and what to say no to. Cheryl Hunter encourages women writing a purpose statement to "Take time for this. Write your mission with help and feedback, and use it. Because not everything has your name on it. Learn to say no."

CAROLYN

When I wrestled with my purpose statement, I had to get clear on where and how I wanted to say yes and to whom I was called. "I coach, speak, and write to equip leaders for Christ" became my guide for what I would say yes and no to. My purpose statement describes how I feel God uses me best. This doesn't mean that I don't sometimes step out of these roles to contribute in other ways, but it does mean most of my work hours are spent coaching, speaking, and writing to equip leaders, as God leads me. In the same way, your purpose statement serves as a guide to help you accomplish the goals and outcomes you desire for your second half.

A Purpose Statement Is Cumulative

Your purpose statement is cumulative because it captures all the work you have done so far.

When Cheryl began writing her purpose statement, she took time to reflect on all the previous work she had done in coaching and to seek the Lord's guidance in prayer and silent meditation. As she reflected on her cumulative halftime work, she asked herself a series of questions as she prepared to craft her statement:

- *Can I trust the Lord in this?* Can I take all this to God in prayer and feel comfortable in where he is leading me?

- *What do I want to do, and who do I want to be?* Do I want to encourage others? Be a mentor? Do I believe God has an assignment and redeployment for me?

- *Whom am I called to serve in my next season?*

Building on her halftime coaching work—her values, passions, strengths, spiritual gifts—and on her intentional time with the Lord in prayer, Cheryl wrote her mission statement:

> I am trusting in the Lord to use my skills to encourage and influence businesspeople who desire to become all God has called them to be, while providing for their families through impacting community and God's Kingdom.

Although it might be a little long for a T-shirt, Cheryl's purpose statement gave her clarity. She went on to accept a position as COO of Open USA, a consulting group supporting businesses that provide jobs and share the gospel in the marketplace. Her assignment is to empower individuals, families, and churches to create businesses that bring spiritual and economic transformation to the least reached. Combining private-sector experience with compassion for the poor, Cheryl also serves on the boards of two nonprofit organizations: Esperanza, a Christian microfinance ministry in the Dominican Republic, and Mission Triangle, a ministry that helps other nonprofits to thrive. Having a purpose statement helped Cheryl protect her calling and provided guiding principles for how she spends her time.

SHAYNE

At the end of my monthly coaching sessions with Carolyn, it was time for me to write my purpose statement. Going through the halftime process had made a huge difference in my life. I had started out feeling disheartened, discouraged, and full of self-pity and doubt. After doing the hard work with Carolyn, I was at a place of enthusiasm and excitement to craft my statement and get going into my second half. Although it was hard at times, it was also fun as I unearthed the Shayne who had been buried under the debris of past hurts and disappointments. I felt more like myself than I had in many years. I had gone dark, but this process not only turned my dreamer back on, it also lifted my depression and anxiety. I again knew who I wanted to be and who I wanted to serve.

A passage from Psalm 27 has great meaning for me. One morning during the darkest time of my life, I reached for my phone and noticed my Bible app was open. I had not opened it and was curious to find it open to Psalm 27:11-14.

> Teach me your way, LORD;
>> lead me in a straight path
>> because of my oppressors.
> Do not turn me over to the desire of my foes,
>> for false witnesses rise up against me,
>> spouting malicious accusations.
> I remain confident of this:
>> I will see the goodness of the LORD
>> in the land of the living.
> Wait for the LORD;
>> be strong and take heart
>> and wait for the LORD.
>
> PSALM 27:11-14, NIV

My eyes teared up, and these verses not only carried me through dark and lonely times but also gave me the strength and faith to wait for the Lord in the confidence that the hard times would end and I would see the goodness of the Lord in the land of the living. My halftime process became my breakthrough to the land of the living. These verses remain deeply meaningful and inform my personal purpose statement:

> I am deeply grounded in my love of God so I can love others free of fear and help other women find their land of the living.

Thanks to the Halftime Institute, Carolyn's coaching, and this process, I am no longer buried in grief, self-pity, and paralysis. Rather, I know who I am and who I want to serve so I can live out my Ephesians 2:10 calling and get going.

CRAFT YOUR PURPOSE STATEMENT

If you've done the work to get clear, get free, and get called, then you are ready to write your purpose statement. Even if you do not feel ready, you *are* ready. It's time to take courage and create the first draft. We say first draft because more likely than not, your purpose statement will change over time as you take your test-drives and discover what fits you best.

Here are three options you can choose from to get started in drafting your purpose statement.

- *Use a template.* Here's one option:
  I am trusting God to use my [*gifts/talents*] to impact and serve [*issue/cause, passions, people group*] in order to [*desired outcome*].

For example:

> I am trusting God to use my *teaching gifts* to impact and serve *underresourced families* in order to *help them escape poverty.*

- *Draw it.* If the words don't flow right away, try capturing it visually first. Draw whatever comes to your mind and heart. Later, you can translate the image to words that capture your purpose statement.

- *Dream write it.* If writing something short and concise feels like a struggle, try "dream writing" your purpose statement. Without worrying about length, describe who you want to be in your second half and who you want to serve. Write until you have no more ideas. When finished, study what you've written and circle the words that most accurately

TROUBLESHOOTING PURPOSE STATEMENT OBSTACLES

If you feel stuck or stalled when it comes to writing your purpose statement, know that you are not alone. Listed below are four common purpose statement obstacles and ways to overcome them.

- **Perfectionism.** Many women have felt hounded by perfectionism their whole lives, and writing something as important as a purpose statement for their entire second half feels daunting. They're plagued by the question, "What if I get it wrong?" The good news is, there is no such thing as a wrong purpose statement. Start by giving yourself grace. Your purpose statement is not chiseled in stone, which means you can change it. Drawing on all you have discovered about yourself, write what makes sense for you today. Then take it one day at a time and make any necessary adjustments to it as you go.

- *Fear of commitment.* The fear of commitment obstacle goes like this: "The second half of life is a long time. How can I write a purpose statement for several decades? That seems impossible." Fortunately, you're not writing a purpose statement that has to remain unchanged for decades. Plus, no one is going to be checking up on you later or grading your outcomes on this draft of your purpose statement. Again, simply write a statement that captures your halftime work to date and makes sense for you today, knowing it may change in the future.

- *Fear of failure.* There is no failure in halftime. Perfectionism and fear of commitment feed this beast: the fear of failure. As you craft your purpose statement, take it to God in prayer. Listen for his voice and promptings and remember, there is no finish line. There are no grades or gold stars. This is a personal and intimate decision between you and God. Give yourself grace by allowing this to be a process—something that develops and changes over time. As long as you're working the process, there is no such thing as failure.

- *Fear of the unattainable.* Some women feel like their dreams and goals are so big that they're actually unattainable. They feel like they should downsize their dreams or choose a different goal. However, if someone has big dreams, we say, "Well done!" Having big dreams means you have engaged the process well. You know who you are and who you want to serve. No matter how audacious your dreams may be, take courage and write them down. You'll never know if they're attainable until you try.

define you and describe your purpose. Use the words you circle to begin writing your concise statement.[4]

Once you complete the first draft of your purpose statement, you may find it helpful to talk it through with a friend or mentor. Or if you have a difficult time writing your statement, you may want to start by having a conversation with a trusted individual who can help you process why you feel stuck.

GOD'S CREATIVE PURPOSES FOR YOU

A key aspect to get going is crafting your personal purpose statement. While some in midlife may attempt to write a purpose statement before really working the process, many individuals struggle with this because they have no idea where to start. Writing your purpose statement at this stage in the process offers you the resources, tools, and knowledge you gained from all your work. Your personal Ephesians 2:10 calling and mission become clear only after the long, prayerful, and intentional process of unpacking who you are today at midlife. It was important to focus on the "being" part of you in

"After twenty-one years with my organization, I left and started my own business. I felt empowered. For the first time in my life, I felt like I was living on mission for God."

Debra Dean, PhD, *organizational leadership*

your dreams, strengths, spiritual gifts, and values before you could attempt to focus on the "doing" part of your second half. Your purpose statement is the total of the work you have done to this point.

Frederick Buechner says, "The place God calls you to is the place where your deep gladness and the world's deep hunger meet."[5] This is your Ephesians 2:10 calling, which includes fulfilling your dreams as well as serving God and others. Your purpose statement brings together your dreams, strengths, gifts, values, life experiences, and desired outcomes into a sentence that defines who you are and whom you serve. Crafting a purpose statement is not an attempt to plan all the specifics of your future life. Instead, as Cheryl says, it is about listening carefully for God's unique assignment and having the courage to write it down. It will help you stay the course to fulfill God's creative purposes for your life.

ESSENTIAL PRACTICES

PRAY

Share. Take out your journal and all the work you have done so far in this halftime process and offer it to the Lord. Share it with him as a silent sacrifice of praise.

Ask. Seek the Lord's guidance by praying through the three questions Cheryl asked as she prepared to craft her purpose statement (page 204).

Listen. God has an assignment and redeployment for your second half. As you prepare to draft your purpose statement, listen for his voice and promptings.

ACT

- Complete the exercise in "Craft Your Purpose Statement" (pages 207–210).

- Briefly review the four common obstacles listed in "Troubleshooting Purpose Statement Obstacles" (pages 208–209).

Overall, how would you assess where you're at when it comes to each obstacle? On each of the continuums below, circle the number that best describes your response.

Perfectionism

1   2   3   4   5   6   7   8   9   10

I do not struggle   I feel paralyzed
with perfectionism.   by perfectionism.

Fear of Commitment

1   2   3   4   5   6   7   8   9   10

I do not struggle   I feel paralyzed
with fear of   by fear of
commitment.   commitment.

Fear of Failure

1   2   3   4   5   6   7   8   9   10

I do not struggle   I feel paralyzed
with fear of failure.   by fear of failure.

Fear of the Unattainable

1   2   3   4   5   6   7   8   9   10

I do not struggle   I feel paralyzed
with fear of the   by fear of the
unattainable.   unattainable.

- Journal your responses to the following questions.

  » Which of the four common obstacles do you struggle with most? Why?

» In what ways, if any, might the obstacles you struggle with be driven by self-limiting beliefs or misguided self-protection?

» Use the power of "What if?" from chapter 9 (pages 182–187) to switch your focus from your obstacle to what's possible. Craft some what-if questions to help you think about your obstacle in a new way. For example, "What if it's okay to be less than perfect?" or "What if I allow myself to have big, audacious dreams?"

ADJUST

Based on what you've learned from taking action, what adjustments do you want to make? Consider any adjustments that will help you overcome your obstacles or will make your purpose statement as effective and accurate as possible.

GET
Part 4
GOING

SHAYNE

It's several years ago now, but I remember the first day of my new job as if it were yesterday. I was sitting in a simple office in a quirky, nearly hundred-year-old building that had few amenities, but I did have a window by my new desk. The sunlight poured in every day, warming my corner and my heart. Giant Midwest pine trees and a sprawling lawn were my views. I had walked to work that morning with a smile on my face, a backpack full of hope, and my laptop. My mantra, *Wait for the Lord*, had changed to *Thank you, thank you, thank you.* Yet, it was deeper than a mere profession of gratitude. When my lips and soul repeated it over and over, I also felt it as *Holy, holy, holy*, as if I were joining the seraphim around the throne who forever sing this hymn of praise. *Thank you, thank you, thank you. Holy, holy, holy.*

This song of praise brought tears to my eyes each day. I had learned to pay attention to my tears of joy, and I was at peace because I knew this was what mattered to me: loving God and being given the opportunity to serve him. I never imagined myself in this full-time job—a job that was not just a paycheck, but the perfect place to launch my second half with purpose. Although much of my halftime journey had been painful and confusing, I now understood I would not be who I am today without those experiences. I knew who I was and who I was not.

Today, I am not afraid—of anything or anyone. I no longer let others' opinions of me sway me from my passions and my purpose. I no longer let other people's agendas override my life, distract me from my mission, or use and abuse me. I no longer let waves of confusion and doubt slam me to the ground. Other people have no say in how I feel about myself and my life. I am free to follow my dreams and my passions, and I will never again apologize for them or silence them. I am a clear thinker, and I know what I know. I trust myself again—and this is no small thing. To relearn this was the fight of my life. As it is with every superhero story, I know that it is the suffering that creates the transformation—the superpowers. I have my superpowers now.

Is it cliché to say that God never left me during the darkest times? Although I had doubted his presence, I now know that in my deep wells of despair, fear, and isolation, God never really left me. He mourned with me, held me as I raged, cried with me, loved me.

On my father's side of the family, we have a tradition. At the end of every family gathering or meal, we sing the classic hymn "Great Is Thy Faithfulness." My grandfather, Joseph, was a simple pastor who ministered in central Indiana. A second-generation immigrant from Germany, he and his wife, Mary, had four children and twenty-seven grandchildren. As our extended family ages and the older generation goes on to glory, this tradition feels more and more intense and emotional—*holy*. Standing in a circle, singing together this sacred hymn, connected by blood and heritage, and with gorgeous harmonies—everyone always tears up. Collectively, this is what matters to us. As a family and as the body of Christ. Together, we know God is faithful.

In my halftime journey, God was faithful to me. The job with the window by the desk was the first step I took into my second half. When I was stuck in self-pity and self-doubt, I had the misconception that it was a job or a title or an accomplishment that was going to enliven my second half and give me joy and purpose. But taking that first step into the unknown was less about a particular role than it was about me getting going. As it turned out, I didn't even need a specific job. I needed my confidence back. I needed to find and live into my purpose again.

All those years ago when God sent me a dream of the ancient, internal well, I knew in my spirit it was significant. And yet, I had not known how this dream and its lessons would continue to be so significant over time. Looking back, I believe God wanted me to know in the depths of my soul that whatever hardships came into my life, an internal well of wide-open spaces—the land of the living, of joy, and of purpose—is what he has always had for me.

Today, I may only be experiencing a tiny glimmer of all he has prepared for me, prepared for all of us, but I can still hear his voice.

"Shayne, it is drawing near! It is coming! It is ancient!"

11

KEEP MOVING DESPITE CONFUSION AND SETBACKS

Let us not become weary in doing good,
for at the proper time we will reap a harvest if we do not give up.

GALATIANS 6:9, NIV

Sharon Kim is no stranger to times of discouragement and confusion. She was born the third of four daughters in a culture that values sons over daughters. When she was just two years old, her parents and oldest sister left South Korea and immigrated to the United States, leaving Sharon and two other sisters behind with a grandmother.

Eventually, she reunited with her parents in the United States, but she and her family continued to experience trauma, including domestic abuse, racism, and bankruptcy. Yet, even in the midst of a chaotic childhood, Sharon sensed God leading her. She felt called to preach to both women and men, even though the latter was frowned upon in her faith tradition.

Despite underlying wounds, confusion, and setbacks, Sharon

persevered and stayed active. She earned a PhD in sociology, and she and her husband planted a church together. Her role at the church was doing most of the administration, strategizing, and discipleship. She was also a devoted mother raising two sons. Then, at age forty, she sensed the Lord saying, *"Sharon, I have a new assignment for you. I want you to stop doing all of the things that you are doing because I have something else for you."*

Sharon did not know what that meant, but she knew she needed to pause and follow God's leading. She and her husband hired others to take over her roles at the church, and she believed her next assignment would show up quickly. It did not. For five years, Sharon was in what she refers to as her midlife "cave of confusion." She was hurting and felt disillusioned. In fact, she felt as if she were at the bottom of a dark pit with no way out.

"For five years, I felt like I was shelved," Sharon recalls. "I was put on the back burner of ministry and didn't know what God had for me. I didn't even know what I was passionate about. There was just a lack of really understanding who I am and what God has called me to do. I felt enveloped by a fog of confusion. In hindsight, though, I realize it was a necessary time."

SOMETIMES THE WAY UP IS DOWN

There will be moments in your halftime journey when you will feel very alone. As Sharon did, you may doubt yourself and wonder where God went. Whether you call it a cave of confusion or a time in the wilderness, when you hit that difficult season it's important to know that you are far from alone. In fact, Halftime Institute coach Jim Dean says, "Every single person who has been through halftime has spent time in this place of confusion, a valley that seems never ending."

Every single person.

No one escapes the proverbial wilderness, and not one of us has had it all together from start to finish. More than a hundred women we interviewed had wilderness experiences during their halftime process. However, what few of us realize when we're in our wilderness season is how necessary it is. It's necessary because sometimes the way up is down.

When you experience setbacks and confusion, it's normal to feel discouraged. There's even a theory with a graph that demonstrates how the way up is, in fact, down. It's called the Sigmoid Curve.

When we begin a new phase of life, there is often an initial decline before growth really takes off. In the diagram below, imagine that the curve represents the transformational growth of an individual.

PERSONAL GROWTH CYCLE

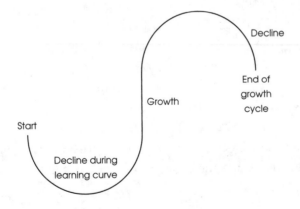

Beginning on the left, a decline in the curve occurs during study and experimentation, which is followed by a sharp move upward during growth and then a decline at the end of the cycle.

Initiating a new curve of growth before the existing one has declined too much is critical to a thriving life.[1]

If you think about it, you've likely already experienced this dynamic multiple times in your life. For example, in the first half of life you may have experienced an initial decline after finishing school and trying to make your way in the world. It took time and effort to find your rhythm, and there were obstacles you had to overcome along the way. But then you hit your stride and things began to move up. You found a job and a spouse, and experienced growth as you made a life for yourself. However, eventually, the curve started to turn down again. You might have hit a new stage of life, such as empty nesting, or made a career move. You might have weathered a tragedy, a broken relationship, or a layoff. Whatever may have caused it, that downward trend is the signal that it's time to initiate the next curve of growth and change.

"I hit what I think was rock bottom. Once there, I leaned completely on the Lord to move forward in life. I began having coffee with God every morning. I was listening instead of constantly speaking. I allowed myself the freedom to be available for whatever God called me to do."

Chris Travelstead, Halftime Institute board member

Here are a few examples of what the initial downward curve—the one that marks the beginning of a new stage of life—might look like.

- *A new job.* Starting a new job is often overwhelming. In addition to learning how to do the job itself, you also have to acclimate to the organizational culture, a new boss, and coworkers. Even when the position is a great fit, you'll likely experience discouragement and self-doubt as you get up to speed.

- *A new skill.* Think back to the last time you had to learn a new skill. Perhaps you took up photography or ballroom dancing, or had to learn how to use a new electronic gadget. In the beginning, you may have considered quitting because it was very clear that you did not yet have the skills you needed. You likely had a dip in your learning curve before you acquired more mastery and began trending upward.

- *A newborn baby.* The first months with a new child, especially a firstborn, are often among the most challenging experiences women face. There are sleepless nights, fears of being solely responsible for this helpless little miracle, and physical changes that make this season especially difficult. If you've had a child, you likely experienced a dip, maybe even postpartum depression, before you hit your stride as a new mom.

But then the curve begins to turn to an upward trajectory.

- *A new job.* You discover your rhythm and master new skills. You understand the culture, your boss, and your coworkers, and you feel encouraged that you are growing and moving up.

- *A new skill.* After you spend some time learning the new system, you may feel in the flow of it. Concepts and techniques begin to click, and you find that this new skill gets easier as you invest time in it. You might also start finding ways to be more creative with your skills.

- *A new baby.* You didn't think it would ever happen, but your little girl finally started sleeping better through the night. You learned how to soothe her, how to interpret her cries, how to make her smile. After those initial challenging months, you began to experience the joys of mothering your child and felt like you were on an upward trajectory.

In all of these scenarios there will eventually be another change or life event that will require you to adjust once again. When the curve of growth and change begins to decline, it's the signal that it's time to initiate a new season of growth and change—a new normal.

There are two inflection points on your Sigmoid Curve. Point A is where you start to wonder if there is more to life than this and what could be next. It is a place of healthy awareness and curiosity. Point B is a classic midlife crisis. Your old way of life is no longer working, and there's no denying it's time for something new.

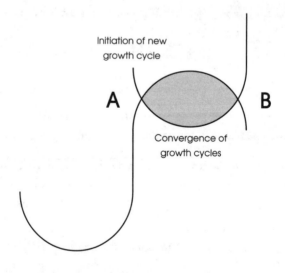

Initiation of new growth cycle

A B

Convergence of growth cycles

The space between points A and B is the transition season, which is where halftime begins. It represents an invitation to get a fresh perspective on your next chapter. And navigating it well could lead to a life change by uncovering deeply buried dreams and passions.

As we've said, this time between the two curves is always challenging. That's why Sharon Kim called it her cave of confusion. However, once she was on the other side, Sharon realized that she had learned some valuable lessons there, and she shared what proved most helpful to her during her season at the bottom of the Sigmoid Curve.

LESSONS FROM THE CAVE OF CONFUSION

Throughout her long transition season, Sharon never stopped praying for direction and wisdom. As she persevered through her hardships, she learned three lessons that were key to eventually moving out of her dark place: She needed to reach out to others, to remember when God had showed up for her in the past, and to go where she was celebrated. Her first step was to reach out to those who were right in front of her, believing God had placed people in her life to help her move forward.

Reach Out

During her time of anxiety and change, God sent Sharon a lifeline. When theologian and author Dallas Willard visited Sharon's church for a conference, he brought along his wife, Jane. Sharon had an instinct that Jane was a divinely arranged connection, and she took a risk to reach out to her even though they had never met before. She told Jane, "I'm really struggling, and I need help."

When Sharon shared her loneliness, loss, and fear, and admitted her need for support and guidance, Jane invited her into a small group she was leading. The group included just two women who

> "My coach helped me take action. I had to get busy removing the obstacles of distraction and confusion before clarity came."
>
> *Debra Dean, PhD, organizational leadership*

eventually became Sharon's closest friends, and Jane became her mentor. Taking the risk to reach out turned out to be a rich experience. These three women provided a wealth of relational support while Sharon was still in her cave of confusion. And the safety and wisdom she experienced in these life-giving relationships eventually helped her move to a new

upward slope on her Sigmoid Curve.

Who might you reach out to for help and support? Who might be right in front of you, a divinely arranged connection?

Remember When God Showed Up

Sharon's midlife crisis was compounded by multiple hardships and challenges. In addition to navigating her own confusion and the legacy of her childhood traumas, her husband was now battling life-threatening health challenges. And yet, even as her problems multiplied, Sharon did not give up hope. Instead, she remembered that God had always been there for her. When she felt confused and uncertain, Sharon remembered times God had brought her peace. When she felt afraid, she remembered times God had brought her to safety.

Even though she was still in her cave of confusion, Sharon knew she needed to keep moving, to keep looking for her new upward curve. Despite uncertainty and discouragement, Sharon anchored herself to God's faithfulness by continually reminding herself of when God had showed up for her in the past—and trusting that he would show up for her again.

When has God showed up for you in the past? What lessons did you learn in those experiences that might help you trust that God will show up for you again?

Go Where You're Celebrated

The light that eventually led Sharon out of her dark cave came when she gave herself permission to operate in her unique strengths and spiritual giftings, and finally began preaching the Word of God to both women and men. She knew she had giftings as a teacher and speaker but had always held herself back to avoid offending others. Although some who were very close to Sharon had contributed to her limiting beliefs by telling her they did not support her preaching, she had the full support of her husband, of her mentor, Jane, and of her close friends.

Rather than focusing on those who didn't support her, Sharon chose to lean into those who did. She did that by going where she was celebrated, not just tolerated. After years of staying small and languishing at the bottom of her Sigmoid Curve, Sharon hit her stride and began the upward trajectory of her second half. She fully stepped into who she was created to be, a preacher, and now she teaches others—women and men—to do the same.

Going where she was celebrated first required that Sharon celebrate herself—the wonderfully made, unique individual that God had created her to be. It required her to embrace the truth that God had created her for a purpose and that staying small did not serve God or her purpose. Going where she was celebrated also required reaching out to others—safe, nonjudgmental individuals in her life who truly appreciated how she was uniquely wired.

Where do you feel that you are tolerated rather than celebrated? What might going where you are celebrated require of you?

WHERE ARE YOU ON THE CURVE?

Take a look at the Sigmoid Curve below and imagine it represents your own halftime experience and process of transformational growth. The goal of this exercise is to give you an idea of where you are now on both the first curve (your current reality), and the second curve (the new growth of your halftime process), and to consider where you hope to be in the year ahead.

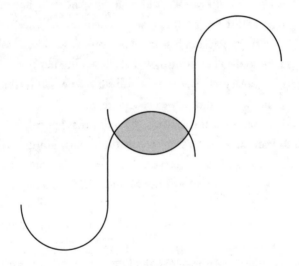

- Starting on the left, the first curve represents the stage of your journey that led you to halftime. Where would you say you are on your current curve? Are you at the beginning and in a place of feeling overwhelmed? Are you on an upward trajectory, learning and mastering new things? Have you reached the intersection point, the place where you feel the curve of your learning and growth turning over on itself, coming to an end? Are you in full-blown transition and decline? Mark an X on the diagram to indicate where you are on the first curve.

• The second curve represents your halftime curve, a new season of growth and change. Where would you say you are on this curve? On the downward slope of the beginning or the upward slope of new learning? Mark an X on the diagram to indicate where you are on the second curve.

• Now consider where you want to be a year from now. For example, you may be in decline on the first curve as your current role is ending but simultaneously be at the beginning of a test-drive opportunity on the second curve. A year from today, you may hope to be higher on the second curve, experiencing new growth and transformation. Mark one more X on the second curve, this one representing where you want to be a year from now.

We hope this exercise encourages you to keep persevering because dips will happen—they are a normal part of change. You will not always be in a place of discouragement, and God is not the author of confusion. He will walk you through your discouragement, safely out of your cave, and stay beside you as you navigate your transition period toward a new calling.

PERSEVERE TO ACTIVATE YOUR CALLING

You will need the power of perseverance to activate your calling. As Sharon Kim and so many others have, you will experience a time of confusion and feel the pain of one season of life ending before another begins. But steady effort forward will make your way clearer.

Perseverance is a frequent theme in the New Testament, especially in the writings of the apostle Paul. He not only understood the power of perseverance in his own calling but consistently encouraged the early Christians to keep going.

- To the Philippians, Paul wrote, "I don't mean to say that I have already achieved these things or that I have already reached perfection. But I press on to possess that perfection for which Christ Jesus first possessed me" (Philippians 3:12).

- To the Galatians Paul wrote, "Let us not become weary in doing good, for at the proper time we will reap a harvest if we do not give up" (Galatians 6:9, NIV).

- To the Corinthians, Paul wrote, "Therefore, since we have this ministry, as we received mercy, we do not lose heart" (2 Corinthians 4:1, NASB).

The apostle James goes so far as reframing hardships as a gift:

Consider it a sheer gift, friends, when tests and challenges come at you from all sides. You know that under pressure, your faith-life is forced into the open and shows its true colors. So don't try to get out of anything prematurely. Let it do its work so you become mature and well-developed, not deficient in any way.

JAMES 1:2-4, MSG

This work of halftime is not only about what you do, but who you are and who you are becoming, God's workmanship. The upward trajectory of your new season will happen if you keep persevering.

ESSENTIAL PRACTICES

PRAY

Share. If you have been in a place of discouragement, bring all your emotions before the Lord. Remember, this transition time is temporary. Share your ideas, your new perspectives, and your hopes for the future.

Ask. As you explore new contexts for your next season, ask for wisdom and perseverance. Ask for guidance and eyes to see the resources, people, and opportunities that may be right in front of you. Ask God to make divine connections, leading you to people who can help you.

Listen. Meditate on what you feel God may be telling you about your next best steps. This part of the journey takes perseverance, so plan to listen and listen again.

ACT

- Complete the exercise in "Where Are You on the Curve?" (pages 228–229).

- Journal your responses to the questions at the end of each section in "Lessons from the Cave of Confusion" (pages 225–228).

ADJUST

Based on what you've learned from Sharon Kim and from taking your own actions, what adjustments do you want to make? How might you adjust your thought process to embrace the power of perseverance as you move forward? Journal any insights.

GO TOGETHER

True transformation happens locally, with others, over time.

BOB BUFORD

Diane Paddison is an achiever with a long list of accomplishments to her name, including a Harvard MBA and stints as a global executive of two Fortune 500 companies and one Fortune 1000 company. However, Diane hit a crossroads at halftime, and the pain of that experience ultimately led her down a new path.

"I was married for eleven years and had two children, but our marriage was no longer what it was supposed to be," Diane says. "Going through a divorce was one of my first major failures, and for an achiever, that alone was a cause of pain—that I totally failed at something. It was hard—really hard. And my children were struggling as well. My son was making bad choices around drugs, alcohol, and sex, and my daughter was very sick. I realized that I was not in control."

Diane was also facing a job transition. Unable to do her job with a healthy work and family balance, she had chosen to resign and, with coaching, decided to take some time to listen and pray rather than jumping into her next thing right away. Diane knew it was the right decision, but she felt very alone in it all.

During her time of pausing, Diane learned that one of the keys to successfully navigating times of transition is seeking wise counsel. Bob Buford called this strategy finding your "islands of health and strength."[1] We call it embracing an inner circle. Your inner circle includes the people who understand you, love you, and have your best interests at heart. They are God-given friends, teachers, and mentors. Diane needed and wanted other women in her life who could supply much-needed health and strength. As the only woman on executive teams in the companies where she worked for twenty-two years, she had always felt alone. Diane also felt alone in the church environment. Church leadership did not know how to use her gifts and strengths beyond nursery duties or potluck planning.

At midlife, Diane craved an authentic community of Christian women. When she couldn't find one, she decided to create one—a place where women around the world could find an inner circle and build relationships. Diane founded 4word, a ministry to connect women and help them reach their God-given potential with confidence. She also wrote a book for women called *Work, Love, Pray: Practical Wisdom for Professional Christian Women and Those Who Want to Understand Them.*

The ministry of 4word provides female mentors to support Christian working women so they do not have to feel isolated in corporate environments. This mentorship program offers professional women the opportunity to receive guidance and perspective from more experienced Christian women who truly care about the work-life-spiritual balance.

"I remember the first testimonial I received," said Diane. "It made me feel as if God had prepared me to be in this exact place where I can impact others. I can help women see that no matter where they are, they are not alone. God is with them, and he is going to use them."

Through Diane's ministry and through mutual connections, Diane met Lisa Payne. You may remember Lisa's story from chapter 8. Lisa discovered she had not just one passion, but three, which she referred to as her pillars: evangelism, fighting poverty through economic development, and opposing human trafficking.

Lisa and Diane began dialoguing about starting a 4word group in Detroit, where Lisa lived. Because Lisa had written a purpose statement around her three pillars, she knew that this ministry fit with her evangelism pillar. In Detroit, she was already meeting with a gathering of about two hundred women dedicated to generous giving called Women Doing Well. She felt God nudging her to extend an invitation to working women who wanted to gather monthly to support other women of faith in the marketplace. Twelve women responded immediately, confirming the need for this group. Lisa reached out to Diane to let her know of the interest, and Diane already had a call set up with Lisa and two other women in order to spearhead the group. The four women connected, and it turned out the two other women and Lisa all went to the same church.

"They're younger," Lisa says. "They're forty. They think I'm their mentor. I think they're my mentors. It's been life-changing to do this together. God set up these connections."

FIND YOUR SECOND-HALF COMMUNITY

Being in community with women who understand you, teach you, encourage you, and cheer for you is essential as you get going. If you do not yet have an inner circle, be encouraged. New friendships and new mentors are out there for you.

Finding like-minded community is critical not only to get going, but to keep going. We are not meant to navigate times of transition alone. This is the time to find and embrace new relationships, to journey together, and to break through to your second half surrounded by women who are on the same journey with you.

> *"God showed me how to take the wisdom he'd given me to help others live in the fullness of their overcomer stories just like he did with mine."*
>
> KP LoveJoy, *founder of LoveJoyCO*

If you are ready to get going and realize you do not have a community, it is a good idea to consider why that might be. One of the things that keeps many women from finding community is fear of competition, comparison, or judgment. For example, one woman we know of stopped attending the Bible study at her church when she was going through a divorce. When another woman in the group noticed her absence and asked the teacher about it, the teacher said, "Maybe she'll be able to come back after she deals with her problems." It's hard not to wonder if the woman had stopped coming because she felt judged.

Women need to be islands of support, health, and strength for one another, but that doesn't always happen. Stay-at-home moms may judge those who chose careers outside the home in their first half, and moms with full-time careers may judge stay-at-home moms for not working outside the home. At this point in our lives, it is good to throw off these false identities and definitions of each other, acknowledge that women come to their halftime from many diverse paths, and open our hearts and lives to relationships with others who share our desire to live out their Ephesians 2:10 calling and get going. Now is the time to set aside assumptions, judgments, anything that divides, and reach out to women who share your passions, calling, and desired context, no matter where they are in their own journey. This spirit of collaboration and community with women from all walks of life starts in our hearts—we have to love our sisters in freedom. Getting rid of judgments and biases about one another is the only way forward if we are going to work together for Kingdom impact.

WHAT TO LOOK FOR IN AN INTENTIONAL COMMUNITY

As you consider gathering an inner circle, it's important to be intentional about whom you invite. This will be your core group, a band of women who will mutually assist one another in decisions about the work and activities each of you will pursue in the next chapter of life. What you're looking for are women who will share wise counsel, provide accountability, be willing to make a commitment, and celebrate one another.

Share wise counsel. A well-formed community fills the need for a source of wise counsel in your life. The wisdom of Scripture is, "By wise guidance you will wage war, and in an abundance of counselors there is victory" (Proverbs 24:6, NASB). In your first half, perhaps you shared too much with the wrong people. One of Carolyn's mentors in business once looked her straight in the eye and said, "You talk too much. You are giving away your power." She now admits he was right. This was a person with the courage to speak truth. When you are looking for those to provide wise counsel in your life, first look at the fruit of their own lives. Are they people who produce the kind of results you hope for in your next season? Search your heart and consider: Do you trust them or is there a check in your spirit? The wise counselors in your life will be truth-tellers.

Provide accountability. In your second half, it is essential to have accountability. Your group should know what you are trying to accomplish and should have permission to ask you about your progress. By placing yourself in intentional community, you are giving the group permission to hold you to your commitments and keep you true to your calling and purpose statement.

Be willing to make a commitment. An effective core group is one whose members are committed to one another. It helps if you share similar interests, calling, and context but that is not essential. The most important thing is that there is a shared understanding that these relationships are real and edifying, and that they pledge to be there for one another. An intentional community is a group of women who are willing to be committed to one another.

Celebrate one another. A well-formed and intentional community should consist of individuals who believe in you, affirm your gifts, and celebrate who you are and who you are becoming. These need to be women you trust and respect. This may or may not include women with whom you have a longtime friendship. The important thing is to consider the women you share your life with and ask yourself: *Do I respect them? Do I trust them? Do they believe in me and celebrate me?* It may be that God is calling you to step back from some relationships that are no longer in alignment with your mission statement.

This inner circle, for wise counsel and accountability, does not have to share your same passions. These are simply friends who will support and help you to make crucial decisions, as you in turn assist and support them. Perhaps these are the same friends who can work through this book together with you. As you move forward, you will also find other friends who share your calling, more divine connections for Kingdom work, just as Diane and Lisa found each other. To be clear, we are not saying you should only have friends who have the same passions, calling, and context. What we are saying is that if your closest community is made up of friends who do not celebrate you, support you, and offer health to your Ephesians 2:10 calling, the role they play in your life may need to be adjusted.

GATHER YOUR INTENTIONAL COMMUNITY

Your final exercise is to do the preliminary work to gather your own intentional community, a small group of women who will walk with you on this journey. Some call this their inner circle; others refer to it as a personal board of directors. Whatever you decide to name your group, the goal is to be wise in choosing the people who will act as your sounding board and steering group. This is your core group, which will assist you in decisions you make about the work and activities you'll pursue in the next chapter of life. These are the people who share your faith and values.

Write down the names. Halftime coach Paul McGinnis offers this guidance for considering who you will gather: "Think of a personal board as a group of individuals who care about you enough to come alongside you during a critical time in order to help you make the most informed, obedient decisions for your next season of life."[2] He suggests jotting down a list of five to seven individuals whom you deeply respect and who genuinely care about you.

Filter your choices through the following questions:

- Who in your network of friends do you consider wise and thoughtful?

- Who do you know who has a similar worldview as you and is not afraid to tell you the truth even when it may not be pleasant?

- Who truly wants the best for you?

- Who might present a different viewpoint?

- Is there anyone who has traversed these waters before you?[3]

Write down the names that come to mind in response to each question. They may be people in your life now or may be from your past—that teacher, mentor, or friend who always seemed to understand you at a deeper level. The people who come to mind when you ask these questions are the ones you need to consider.

Decide whether you will meet one-on-one with each person or meet as a group. Next, think through how you want to engage with your intentional community. Paul McGinnis decided not to convene his personal board of directors in a group meeting but rather to meet individually with each person, either face-to-face or online, at least once a month. He also committed to updating the entire group monthly via email to ensure everyone stayed on the same page. Paul chose to meet one-on-one because all of his inner-circle members were local, and he saw more value in the insights of the individuals than he did in the group's view as a whole. Others have chosen to bring their intentional community together as a group at specific intervals. The benefits of meeting together include being able to brainstorm solutions, work through confusion as a group, and share feedback. You will know what makes the most sense for you and the individuals on your list.

Be honest about your journey and communicate why you need each person's help. State clearly what you are struggling with and how you hope each person might help you. For example, "I am considering some different paths forward in a process called 'women at halftime.' I would appreciate your wise counsel, honest feedback, and prayers going forward. Most of all, I hope we can have fun in this adventure." You may also wish to specify a time limit. For example, you could say that you are looking for a six-month commitment of monthly meetings. If you are meeting as a group for mutual support, make sure your relationships are reciprocal, that you are praying for the other members of your intentional community and giving back in the ways they need help. This group of God-given friends has the potential to keep you going when you are stuck, to encourage you when you face challenges, and to be the divine connection that moves you forward when you are stalled.

CELEBRATE TOGETHER

Our goal in writing *Women at Halftime* was to give you a proven process to find joy and purpose in your second half of life. Following are testimonies from women just like you who did the hard work and dug up their clogged wells as they leaned into their new Ephesians 2:10 calling. They found their islands of strength and hope in one another. We share them as celebration stories in the hope that they will encourage you.

- "I have more faith now than I ever have—not because I am certain but because I am uncertain, and I am leaning into the power of mystery and vulnerability. I am realizing wisdom comes from listening."
  —*Mercedes D. Tucker, director of development and connection for Project I See You*

- "In my second half I feel peaceful, grateful, thoughtful, purposeful, loved, enthusiastic, and exhilarated. I am now defined by a résumé of God-allowed experiences, opportunities, hurts, and lessons that have equipped me to do the job God created me to do."
  —*Chris Travelstead, Halftime Institute board member*

- "I'm now in my midsixties, a time when most of my friends are retiring, playing golf, and traveling. Yet God opened a door so wide that my husband and I said yes to his call to move to Southeast Asia. We now live in a developing country and pour out on others all the love that God has poured into us. It is an incredible journey, a joyful journey."
  —*Katherine Huske, senior marketing executive*

- "My halftime journey gave me tools, a plan, and relationships to see what God has for me. Nowhere in Scripture does it tell us to retire when we hit fifty or sixty. In fact, that may be when we can do some of our greatest work. That was just

a profound shift for me. No matter what has happened in the past, you can move forward and have an impact."
—*Wende Gaikema, ICF certified executive coach*

It is our hope that you are now well on your way to moving from the crises and challenges of midlife to a meaningful and abundant second half full of joy and purpose. When we began this journey together, we started by focusing on your dreamer, your true self, your values, and unpacking who you are at the soul level. Next, we challenged you to address any obstacles that might prevent you from accomplishing your dreams. Then we led you through a process of rediscovering your passions, finding what fits you, and writing a purpose statement. And now the goal is to build on all the work you've already done to get going on your second half.

We hope you are taking steps to get going with your Ephesians 2:10 calling, living a life of joy and purpose as you embrace who God has made you to be in order to love and serve him and others.

"To women who have heard God's whisper to pivot in a new direction, I say, 'May you take care of your soul, let go of the weight of what others think you should be doing, find your peace, and be at ease with the inner wisdom that knows what is best for you.'"

Virginia Sambuco, former customer care executive

Now is the time to celebrate the wide-open space of your second half with a strong community, and with friends who also desire to live their second half with purpose. And remember, your transformational journey is not something that ends. As long as you're on this earth, the journey of growth and transformation continues. Continue to pray, act, and adjust as you increasingly become the person God has created you to be. Today, celebrate where you are and keep walking forward.

ESSENTIAL PRACTICES

PRAY

Share. Open up to God about the women in your life. Share with him any pain or disappointments around these relationships and share with him the desires of your heart about your dreams for your second-half community.

Ask. Ask God to bring women into your life who will provide wise counsel, assist you with decision-making, be willing to make a commitment, and celebrate you as you pursue your second half with joy and purpose.

Listen. Open your heart to God's promptings, listening for the names of those to whom you can reach out to cultivate an inner circle of support and community.

ACT

- Complete the exercise described in "Gather Your Intentional Community" (pages 239–241).

- Write a one-paragraph testimony or celebration story summarizing the most important thing you've learned or experienced so far on your halftime journey.

ADJUST

Based on what you've learned about gathering a community for your second half, what adjustments do you want to make?

Consider any fine-tuning of relationships or community that could help you get going and keep going. Act on these adjustments and continue to keep an open heart for those God has out there for you—other women to join you in your wide-open spaces, in your new joy and purpose.

IT'S NEVER TOO LATE

Linda Buford

I married my hero, the late Texas entrepreneur Bob Buford, whom *Christianity Today* called the "Christian leader's leader."[1] As a person of influence, Bob was a humble and gentle man. Following Bob's passing, Bob Roberts Jr. wrote this tribute:

> No one believed in me more and expected less in return than Bob Buford; he only wanted me to bear much fruit. When Bob lost his son, he became a father to hundreds of other sons and daughters in the form of pastors and business leaders whose lives and ministries he spoke into.
>
> People look at Bob as a businessman who used his money to advance the kingdom, but he was much, much more than a businessman.[2]

As Bob's wife, I can tell you all these words are true. Bob never sought accolades for himself and never expected a legacy. Before storms hit our life, we had a picture-book life. We had a handsome, popular son. We traveled the world with the Young Presidents' Organization. We had a big house, beautiful Christian friends, a great church, and many parachurch experiences, and Bob was able to reach his professional goals early in life. In 1994, Bob wrote a bestselling book called *Halftime: Moving from Success to Significance*, which greatly influenced many Christian leaders, both in the marketplace and in full-time ministry.

The book *Halftime* is Bob's story, and he wrote it for men who were very much like him. They were businessmen doing well and getting to a certain stage of life, and he was concerned about them. Many were falling into lifestyles centered around money or pleasure, and many were going through divorce and other life challenges. Bob wanted to encourage these men to become more philanthropic and mission focused—to make their lives matter.

The *Halftime* book and the Halftime Institute that grew from it offered a tailored and intentional process to encourage individuals to take stock of their life and to chart a new course for their second half. At its inception, the halftime process was designed for men. Yet, many wives soon realized it was a package deal. If your spouse was in halftime, so were you. You could not separate the two because you live with the outcomes of your husband's decisions for his life.

Although I was married to Bob and experienced his halftime, it was always evident to me that my life story, my experience at halftime, was very different. Much of my life was about adapting to transitions and different seasons of life. Much of my journey was about navigating how his life choices affected my life and my identity.

In his forties, Bob was very interested in the Bible, and he felt called to do something more than his business ventures. He felt he had done what he was supposed to do as CEO of Buford Television, Inc., a business started by his mother. It began with a single ABC affiliate in Tyler, Texas, and grew into a national network of cable systems. It was a family company, and he was in charge. As the oldest of three sons, Bob felt he had done a good job for his brothers.

Bob began a ministry parallel to his television career. However, things began to get exhausting when he was doing both. He was not around much during this time, so I managed everything at home. Plus, we had a farm, and I managed all the people who worked for us there. I wanted to create an island of peace for Bob when he was home.

Bob eventually scaled back the time he spent in business and began dedicating more time to philanthropy and ministry. He taught Sunday school, joined the board of directors for a Christian camp, and worked with young people and other groups. Yet he still had an itch to do something big.

During this time, Bob, like so many people at halftime, felt confused and unfocused. A now famous story of Bob's life, and a favorite story of the Halftime Institute, centers around a meeting he had with a strategic planning consultant named Mike Kami. However, there's an important part of this story—my part—that has never been told.

WHAT'S IN THE BOX?

During their first meeting, Mike challenged Bob to get very clear on what mattered most to him, where he could be most helpful, and how he could invest his time, talents, and treasure. Then he asked Bob this crucial question: "What's in the box?" In other words, "What one thing matters most to you?"

Here is what Bob wrote about that conversation.

[Mike] announced that we could not put together an honest plan for my life until I identified the mainspring. "I've been listening to you for a couple of hours," he said, "and I'm going to ask you what's in the box. For you, it is either money or Jesus Christ. If you can tell me which it is, I can tell you the strategic planning implications of that choice. If you can't tell me, you are going to oscillate between those two values and be confused."

No one had ever put such a significant question to me so directly. After a few minutes (which seemed like hours), I said, "Well, if it has to be one or the other, I'll put Jesus Christ in the box."[3]

For Bob, this was a commitment to acknowledge Christ as his guiding light, a promise to follow God wherever he led.

I was present during that two-hour meeting between Bob and Mike and heard every word. I heard Mike say, "You've been vacillating between money and success and your faith." He did indeed tell Bob that he had to decide what was in that box—and Bob put a cross in the box.

I sat in silence and listened in shock. I did not know what Bob's response meant at the time, but I knew my life was about to change. It eventually meant Bob got out of the television business, sold the company, and put that money into God's Kingdom work. I was not against it; I was just numb.

I thought, *Who am I if I'm no longer the CEO's wife? I'm not a* minister's wife. *Will we move to a smaller house? Will we give away everything? Will we no longer go to nice restaurants?* Some of my concerns may seem silly, but I was younger and feared we would be giving up everything we had worked for.

Bob's sudden decision was made without me, and yet it affected my whole life. It launched me into a season of having to trust that God knew what Bob was doing. Of course, he did, but God didn't let me in on it right away, and I had a lot of fear.

A SEASON OF STORMS

My halftime journey was not about hitting a certain age or any sort of midlife crisis. Loss and change rolled through my life like a season of storms. First was Bob's mother, a force in his life, in *our* life. Bob's mother had grown up in East Texas in the small town of Henderson, near Tyler. Lucille was a woman before her time, with a journalism education from the University of Missouri, along with radio broadcasting experience. As a single mom with an eye toward the future, she had heard about television and thought it would be "a coming thing."

In 1954, Tyler was a growing, midsize city and that was where she bought her first television station. And she did it as a woman, alone. Four people had applied for a license to get the Tyler station: a newspaperman, a big oilman, a banker, and Lucille. And Lucille got it. It was shocking at the time. Lucille was a little lady with a radio station and three sons, and she somehow beat out the three men to start KLTV. The *L* stands for Lucille.

Bob and his mom had a unique relationship. He used to say his mother read him profit-and-loss statements rather than fairy tales, and she gave him a briefcase when he was just twelve years old. Bob was the oldest, and most likely she felt that if he was able to learn the important business lessons at a young age, he could then help his brothers, which is exactly what happened. Lucille gave Bob freedom to make mistakes and didn't interfere as he learned everything from writing commercials to selling airtime. He became the manager of KLTV while she was still living. She was a strong and remarkable presence in his life.

In 1971, about five years after we were married, Lucille died in a hotel fire. Her tragic death was the first storm we faced.

The next big storm was losing Ross, our only son, at age twenty-four when he and two of his friends attempted to swim the Rio Grande River, which separates South Texas from Mexico. They wanted to understand what immigrants faced when they attempted this journey to freedom. One young man made it across. Ross and the other friend did not.

Unthinkably, I had lost a brother just a few months before losing Ross. My brother had encephalitis, and we never found out how he contracted it. I felt overwhelmed by loss.

Ross's death was reported in the newspapers and on television. The story was picked up by the Associated Press and a lot of city newspapers. People started calling to comfort me, and when they did, I found they often also shared their own losses. Many had lost a loved one or had problems with their children, and I ended up being someone they could talk to.

It was tender how God used me during that season of bereavement, but I was sad for a long time. The reality going forward was that my family was now just Bob and me. That was it. I would never have grandchildren. Yet, I did not crumble, and I know that was the Lord upholding me, and the people who surrounded me. God was with me all the way and every day.

A few months after we lost Ross, one of Bob's brothers died

in a freak accident. And then my aging parents needed me in San Antonio. With my brother gone, I was now an only child, and it was up to me to split my time taking care of them and their business, while also caring for Bob.

After Ross died, we moved to Dallas, which was another loss. I left behind my Share Group at church, my loving Christian friends, my support system, and God's people who had gotten me through losing Ross.

Despite bearing witness to the creation of the Halftime Institute, I have never felt as if my own story was a traditional halftime story. I did not have a platform for influence or a ministry of my own because I had a life sidelined by storms and caretaking.

THE BIGGEST STORM

The biggest storm in my life was losing Bob. His illness came on gradually. It started about two years before anyone else but me knew about it. We went to the Mayo Clinic and received confirmation that it was a degenerative problem and that there was no cure. His illness lasted about six years, and it was very difficult toward the end.

We had two funeral services—one in Tyler where Ross was buried, and another a few months later in Dallas, which was for pastors and others in ministry who came from across the country to honor Bob. That period between the burial in April and the bigger funeral in mid-June was especially difficult because I could not get a sense of closure.

Throughout all these storms, the people at the Halftime Institute were so kind. They regularly checked on me and continue to talk with me about a purpose and a renewed plan for my life. Now, at age eighty, I cannot help but wonder, *Haven't those years passed me by?* Yet, I wake up every day with the same thought as women of other ages: *Now what?*

After the storm of Bob's death, I went through a spiritual drought and a hard season. I had needed hip surgery for years but didn't want to have it while Bob was sick. After his funerals, I had the surgery, but it went wrong, and I had to go in for a second surgery just a couple of weeks later. This depleted me for a long time while I dealt with physical therapy as well as two years of probate to settle financial and legal details following Bob's death.

Once again, I didn't crumble, and God's people were there for me.

As it turned out, I ended up discovering a renewed sense of purpose when Bob left me in charge of the Buford Foundation. If you can have halftime at eighty, I did. I've had a new season of transition as far as genuinely turning to something I'm interested in and feeling as if it is a "God thing."

I am enjoying this season of my life very much. I am not interested in leaving a legacy. I simply want to be useful in God's Kingdom and to do his will and use his money wisely. I have never felt closer to God, and I talk to him all the time. It's never too late to do something big in life, and I want to contribute until the day I die. I am not finished.

ACKNOWLEDGMENTS

With profound appreciation and respect, we are thankful for the late Bob Buford, who began the movement of the Halftime Institute with his book, *Halftime: Moving from Success to Significance.*

We give thanks to the Halftime Institute, which is supporting a new narrative of women's voices at midlife. The Halftime Institute in Dallas serves thousands of clients in the United States, Canada, Australia, Singapore, Hong Kong, and South Africa, and continues to expand globally in order "to turn the latent energy of American Christianity into active energy."[1] Buford's vision is growing, and today the Halftime Institute serves both men and women. We are thankful for the opportunity to build on Buford's original vision and passion and for the opportunity to write this book for the needs of women at halftime.

This book could not have been written without the contributions of more than one hundred women who took part in our surveys, participated in women's advisory calls, and shared their stories with us. The authenticity and vulnerability of this diverse group of women cannot be overstated.

Many thanks also go to the Halftime Institute board of directors and staff, including cofounder Lloyd Reeb, chairman of the board Dean Niewolny, and vice president of admissions Dr. Rhonda Kehlbeck. Lloyd, Dean, and Rhonda all believe in raising up women at midlife, and each of them contributed stories and input.

The idea for this book began in a conversation with a client and now board member, Cecilia Fileti. The idea went on to be supported by Halftime Institute directors Margie Blanchard and Chris Travelstead, and others who now lead the Halftime Institute.

We wish to express gratitude to our agent, Don Gates, founder and president of the Gates Group, who embraced the project from day one and who found the perfect home for this book with the outstanding team at Tyndale House Publishers. Jan Long Harris, Sarah Atkinson, Carol Traver, Andrea Martin, and the entire team at Tyndale Momentum are committed to publishing conversation-starting books that address real-life issues. Finally, we want to thank our editor, Christine Anderson, who helped us dig deep, clarify, and refine this message of hope. We hope this book will be just the start of a new conversation and a new group of women who feel freed to embrace their Ephesians 2:10 calling:

> *We are His workmanship, created in Christ Jesus*
> *for good works, which God prepared beforehand*
> *so that we would walk in them.*

NOTES

INTRODUCTION: WELCOME TO HALFTIME

1. Annette Joan Thomas, Ellen Sullivan Mitchell, and Nancy Fugate Woods, "The Challenges of Midlife Women: Themes from the Seattle Midlife Women's Health Study," *Women's Midlife Health* 4, no. 8 (June 15, 2018): https://doi.org/10.1186/s40695-018-0039-9.

2. Louann Brizendine, *The Female Brain* (New York: Three Rivers Press, 2006), 155.

3. Elizabeth Arias et al., "Provisional Life Expectancy Estimates for 2020," *Vital Statistics Rapid Release*, Report No. 15, July 2021, US Department of Health and Human Services, Centers for Disease Control and Prevention, https://www.cdc.gov/nchs/data/vsrr/vsrr015-508.pdf.

4. Lynnette Leidy Sievert, Nicole Jaff, and Nancy Fugate Woods, "Stress and Midlife Women's Health," *Women's Midlife Health* 4, no. 4 (March 16, 2018): https://doi.org/10.1186/s40695-018-0034-1.

5. Bahar Gholipour, "Middle-Age Women Have Highest Rate of Depression," LiveScience, December 3, 2014, https://www.livescience.com/48978 -middle-age-women-highest-depression-rate.html.

6. Carina Storrs, "U.S. Suicide Rates Up, Especially among Women, but Down for Black Males," CNN, April 22, 2016, https://www.cnn.com/2016 /04/22/health/suicide-rates-rise/index.html.

7. David G. Blanchflower, "Is Happiness U-Shaped Everywhere? Age and Subjective Well-Being in 132 Countries," National Bureau of Economic Research, January 2020, https://www.nber.org/papers/w26641.

8. Jo Hemmings, Rachel Halliwell, and Samantha Brick, "Crippling Debts, Crumbling Relationships, Left Behind at Work, Needy Children and Parents: Why More and More Middle-Aged Women Say Life Feels Like a Burden," *Daily Mail*, August 23, 2018, https://www.dailymail.co.uk/femail/article-6087639/Why-middle-aged-women-say-life-feels-like-burden.html.

9. Although *Women at Halftime* is not part of the Halftime Institute's official coaching curriculum, we draw on Halftime Institute principles and share stories of many women we've coached over the years. We are grateful for the Halftime Institute's support and partnership in our work. To learn more about Halftime Institute programs and coaching, visit https://halftimeinstitute.org.

CHAPTER 2: TURN YOUR DREAMER BACK ON

1. Brené Brown, *Daring Greatly: How the Courage to Be Vulnerable Transforms the Way We Live, Love, Parent, and Lead* (New York: Avery Penguin Random House, 2012), 32.

CHAPTER 3: RECLAIM YOUR TRUE SELF

1. Ruthellen Josselson, *Revising Herself: The Story of Women's Identity from College to Midlife* (New York: Oxford University Press, 1996), 27.

2. NASB.

3. "Poiema—Greek Word Study," Preceptaustin, September 24, 2012, https://preceptaustin.wordpress.com/2012/09/24/poiema-greek-word-study/.

4. We encourage all the women we coach to take the CliftonStrengths assessment. To learn more, visit https://www.gallup.com/cliftonstrengths/en/253868/popular-cliftonstrengths-assessment-products.aspx.

5. Jim Asplund, "How Your Strengths Set You Apart," Gallup, November 5, 2021, https://www.gallup.com/cliftonstrengths/en/356810/strengths-set-apart.aspx.

6. Tom Rath, *StrengthsFinder 2.0* (New York: Gallup Press, 2007), 20.

7. Eric Liddell, quoted by Eric Geiger, "I Feel God's Pleasure When I . . . ," Eric Geiger blog, March 17, 2014, https://ericgeiger.com/2014/03/i-feel-gods-pleasure-when-i-blank/.

8. "Learn about the Science of CliftonStrengths," Gallup, https://www.gallup.com/cliftonstrengths/en/253790/science-of-cliftonstrengths.aspx.

9. Rath, *StrengthsFinder 2.0*, 37–172.

10. "The History of CliftonStrengths," Gallup, https://www.gallup.com
/cliftonstrengths/en/253754/history-cliftonstrengths.aspx.

11. Cori Shaff and Emily Hoyt, "The CliftonStrengths: Focusing on Strengths
as a Predictor of Success," *Career Development Network Journal* 33, no. 4
(Winter 2017–2018): 75.

12. "Your Spiritual Gifts: How to Identify and Effectively Use Them," *Unfolding
Faith* (blog), accessed December 2, 2021, https://www.tyndale.com/sites
/unfoldingfaithblog/2018/11/13/your-spiritual-gifts-how-to-identify-and
-effectively-use-them/.

13. Charles Stanley, "About Spiritual Gifts: How Can I Discover My Spiritual
Gifts?," *Believers Bible Study*, accessed December 2, 2021, https://
believersgarifunaministriesbible.weebly.com/by-dr-charles-stanley.html.

14. SpiritualGiftsTest.com offers a free online assessment. See "Spiritual Gifts
Test: Adult Version," https://spiritualgiftstest.com/spiritual-gifts-test
-adult-version/.

15. *Merriam-Webster*, s.v. "environment," accessed December 2, 2021,
https://www.merriam-webster.com/dictionary/environment.

CHAPTER 4: IDENTIFY YOUR VALUES

1. Steven C. Hayes, "10 Signs You Know What Matters," *Psychology Today*,
September 2018, https://www.psychologytoday.com/us/articles/201809
/10-signs-you-know-what-matters.

2. Daniel Goleman, *Emotional Intelligence: Why It Can Matter More than IQ*
(New York: Bantam Books, 1995, 2006), 4.

3. Stacy Liberatore, "Average Person Has Over 6,000 Thoughts per Day,
according to Study That Isolated a 'Thought Worm' in the Human Brain
Showing When an Idea Begins and Ends," *Daily Mail*, July 16, 2020,
https://www.dailymail.co.uk/sciencetech/article-8531913/Average-person
-6-000-thoughts-day-according-study-isolated-thought-worm.html.

4. "What Is Emotional Intelligence?," Genos International, accessed December
2, 2021, https://www.genosinternational.com/emotional-intelligence/.

5. "What Is Emotional Intelligence?," Genos International.

6. Bob Buford, *Halftime: Moving from Success to Significance* (Grand Rapids,
MI: Zondervan, 1994, 2008), 37.

CHAPTER 5: LEAVE BEHIND FEARS AND LIMITING BELIEFS

1. "Pairing and Expanding Your Strengths: Strategic," CliftonStrengths,
Gallup, November 3, 2016, https://www.gallup.com/cliftonstrengths/en
/250493/pairing-expanding-strengths-strategic.aspx.

2. Jordan W. Smoller et al., "Prevalence and Correlates of Panic Attacks

in Postmenopausal Women: Results from an Ancillary Study to the Women's Health Initiative," *Archives of Internal Medicine* 163, no. 17 (September 22, 2003): 2041–50, https://pubmed.ncbi.nlm.nih.gov /14504117/.

CHAPTER 6: CREATE CAPACITY FOR YOUR NEW PATH FORWARD

1. Vocabulary.com, s.v. "capacity," accessed December 3, 2021, https:// www.vocabulary.com/dictionary/capacity.
2. Bob Buford, *Halftime: Moving from Success to Significance* (Grand Rapids, MI: Zondervan, 1994, 2008), 132.
3. John Ortberg, *The Life You've Always Wanted: Spiritual Disciplines for Ordinary People* (Grand Rapids, MI: Zondervan, 2002), 76–77.
4. Henry Cloud, *Necessary Endings: The Employees, Businesses, and Relationships That All of Us Have to Give Up in Order to Move Forward* (New York: HarperCollins, 2010), 8.

CHAPTER 7: EMBRACE FORGIVENESS

1. C. S. Lewis, *Mere Christianity* (San Francisco, CA: HarperOne, 1952, 1980), 115.
2. Lewis B. Smedes, AZ Quotes, https://www.azquotes.com/quote/758956.
3. C. S. Lewis, *Mere Christianity*, 115–16.
4. Burt Helm, "This Founder Left an Abusive Marriage at 18. Then She Launched 2 Multimillion-Dollar Companies," *Inc.* magazine, July/August, 2017, https://www.inc.com/magazine/201707/burt-helm/tana-greene -blue-bloodhound-trucking-company.html.
5. The mission of Safe Alliance is to provide hope and healing to those impacted by domestic violence and sexual assault. One in three women will be affected by sexual assault or domestic violence during their lifetime. To learn more about Safe Alliance, visit www.safealliance.org.
6. Nancy Colier, "What Is Forgiveness and How Do You Do It?," *Psychology Today*, March 15, 2018, https://www.psychologytoday.com/us/blog/inviting -monkey-tea/201803/what-is-forgiveness-and-how-do-you-do-it.
7. Beth Moore (@BethMooreLPM), Twitter, December 21, 2016, https:// twitter.com/BethMooreLPM/status/811565696920547329.
8. Mayo Clinic Staff, "Forgiveness: Letting Go of Grudges and Bitterness," Mayo Clinic, November 13, 2020, https://www.mayoclinic.org/healthy -lifestyle/adult-health/in-depth/forgiveness/art-20047692.
9. Matthew 6:9-13, as quoted in *The Book of Common Prayer* (New York: Church Publishing, Inc., 1979), 97.

CHAPTER 8: TAKE THE PULSE OF YOUR PASSIONS

1. Walter A. Elwell, "Purpose," *Evangelical Dictionary of Biblical Theology* (Grand Rapids, MI: Baker Books, 1997), accessed via Bible Study Tools, https://www.biblestudytools.com/dictionaries/bakers-evangelical-dictionary /purpose.html.
2. Søren Kierkegaard, *Papers*, quoted in Ronald M. Green, *Kierkegaard and Kant: The Hidden Debt* (Albany, NY: State University of New York, 1992), 1.
3. *The Halftime Coaching Companion* (Irving, TX: The Halftime Institute, 2014), 13.
4. Rick Warren, *The Purpose Driven Life* (Grand Rapids, MI: Zondervan, 2002, 2011, 2012), 5.

CHAPTER 9: DISCOVER WHAT FITS YOU

1. The Halftime Institute uses the term "low-cost probe" (LCP) to describe this process. A low-cost probe is an intentionally designed, limited test-drive that aligns with your true identity, values, passions, and capacity. It is designed to enable you to assess what fits you in this new season of life. *The Halftime Coaching Companion* (Irving, TX: The Halftime Institute, 2014), 111–113.

CHAPTER 10: WRITE A PURPOSE STATEMENT

1. Peter F. Drucker, *The Five Most Important Questions You Will Ever Ask about Your Organization* (San Francisco: Jossey-Bass, 2008), 14.
2. Fred R. David and Forest R. David, *Strategic Management Concepts and Cases: A Competitive Advantage Approach, Concepts and Cases*, 16th ed. (Essex, England: Pearson Education, 2016), 160.
3. William Strunk Jr. and E. B. White, *The Elements of Style*, 4th ed. (Hoboken, NJ: Pearson Education, 1935, 1999), 29.
4. *The Halftime Coaching Companion* (Irving, TX: The Halftime Institute, 2014), 44–54.
5. Frederick Beuchner, *Wishful Thinking: A Seeker's ABC*, cited in the magazine *Third Way* 17, no. 5 (June 1994): 24.

CHAPTER 11: KEEP MOVING DESPITE CONFUSION AND SETBACKS

1. Rebecca O. Bagley, "The Key to Growth: Transformational Change," *Forbes*, January 2, 2013, https://www.forbes.com/sites/rebeccabagley /2013/01/02/the-key-to-growth-transformational-change/?sh =29ce18066b8c.

CHAPTER 12: GO TOGETHER

1. Bob Buford, *Halftime: Moving from Success to Significance* (Grand Rapids, MI: Zondervan, 1994, 2008), 131.
2. Paul McGinnis, "How to Create Your Personal Board of Directors," LinkedIn, May 18, 2017, https://www.linkedin.com/pulse/how-create -your-personal-board-directors-paul-mcginnis.
3. McGinnis, "How to Create Your Personal Board of Directors."

AFTERWORD: IT'S NEVER TOO LATE

1. Kate Shellnutt, "Remembering Bob Buford, the Christian Leader's Leader," *Christianity Today*, April 19, 2018, https://www.christianitytoday .com/news/2018/april/bob-buford-died-leadership-network-halftime -peter-drucker.html.
2. Bob Roberts Jr., quoted in Shellnutt, "Remembering Bob Buford."
3. Bob Buford, *Halftime: Moving from Success to Significance* (Grand Rapids, MI: Zondervan, 1994, 2008), 53–54.

ACKNOWLEDGMENTS

1. *The Halftime Coaching Companion* (Irving, TX: The Halftime Institute, 2014), 54.

ABOUT THE AUTHORS

Shayne Moore is the author of five books, including *Ending Human Trafficking* and *Women at Halftime*. Her book about modern-day slavery, *Refuse to Do Nothing*, received the Resource of the Year award from *Outreach Magazine*. Her first book, *Global Soccer Mom*, chronicles her work with the HIV/AIDS pandemic. Shayne holds an MA in theology and earned a certificate in screenwriting at UCLA's School of Theater, Film, and Television. She is also contributing editor for *Everbloom: Stories of Living Deeply Rooted and Transformed Lives*. Shayne and her husband, John, now empty nesters, reside in Dallas, Texas.

Carolyn Castleberry Hux is a former journalist and cohost of *Living the Life* on ABC Family Channel. She found her second-half calling coaching women and national security teams for transformational change. Carolyn is an executive coach, a Gallup-Certified Strengths Coach, and a Genos Emotional Intelligence practitioner. She is the author of several positive change books, including *It's About Time! 10 Smart Strategies to Avoid Time Traps and Invest Yourself Where It Matters*. Carolyn and her husband, Ernie, live in Virginia Beach, Virginia, and have a blended family of five grown children and three grandchildren. For fun, they love to spend time on their boat, aptly named *Gratitude*.

HALF|TIME

If you liked this book, you'll want to keep gaining clarity and build connections with other women like you!

Free yourself from the uncertainty of going it alone by connecting with other women experiencing this midlife phenomenon of halftime. Tap into inner confidence and enduring joy as you are propelled by others' support, friendship, and inspiration—and help them do the same!

Explore opportunities for deeper discovery at womenathalftime.org.

Embrace the joy of activating a future so compelling you *can't not* bring it to life. And know that you'll have the support and community you need every step of the way.

Never feel alone or defeated on your journey again—join us today!